JOHN RYAN'S EXPRESS

ONE OF THE UK'S LARGEST O GAUGE LAYOUTS

JOHN RYAN AND PETER TUFFREY

FOREWORD BY PETE WATERMAN

GREAT NORTHERN

Great Northern Books Limited
PO Box 1380, Bradford, BD5 5FB
www.greatnorthernbooks.co.uk

© Peter Tuffrey 2019

Every effort has been made to acknowledge correctly and contact the copyright holders of material in this book. Great Northern Books Ltd apologises for any unintentional errors or omissions, which should be notified to the publisher.

All rights reserved. No part of this book may be reproduced in any form or by any means without permission in writing from the publisher, except by a reviewer who may quote brief passages in a review.

ISBN: 978-1-912101-49-8

Photography by Tristram Tuffrey [unless stated]

Design and layout: David Burrill

CIP Data
A catalogue for this book is available from the British Library

ACKNOWLEDGEMENTS

Tony Bagwell, Karl Crowther, David Dippie, Brian Lewis, Hugh Parkin, Pete Rawlinson, Bill Reed, Mike Sant, Kevin Tams, Cliff Williams, Tony Wright.
Special thanks to Norman Solomon for help and advice throughout the project.

Unless otherwise stated all archive photographs from Peter Tuffrey collection.

CONTENTS

FOREWORD
PETE WATERMAN..................4

CHAPTER ONE
BEGINNINGS..........................6

CHAPTER TWO
LAYING TRACK.....................16

CHAPTER THREE
LOCOMOTIVES....................58

CHAPTER FOUR
CARRIAGES........................118

CHAPTER FIVE
WAGONS............................154

FOREWORD

PETE WATERMAN

Music writer and rail enthusiast, Pete Waterman, on a visit to Keighley and Worth Valley Railway, Oakworth, December, 2003. Reproduced courtesy of Yorkshire Post Newspapers.

John Ryan shares with me an undying passion for model railways. In our childhood days we were captivated by locomotives hurtling past us, powerful but filthy, in the last gasp of steam during the austere 1950s. Since that time we have tried to painstakingly recreate those lost magical moments in our model railway layouts. John and I have been successful in our various businesses and we have both been bold enough to heavily invest in a hobby that has no relationship to them. That is the wonder and craziness of model railways. But neither of us has any regrets. We've enjoyed every penny spent.

Of course it was natural for John to concentrate his attention on modelling locomotives seen in his early days around Doncaster, which is noted as a famous railway centre. The 'Plant' Works was responsible for building *Flying Scotsman* and *Mallard*. We both have our parents to thank for our introduction to railways. John's dad took him to watch A4s, A3s, A1s and A2s passing regularly through the Doncaster station area and my mother used to leave me on Leamington Spa station so I could observe a fantastic array of engines from that viewpoint.

John's present layout has evolved passionately over a number of years and although not modelled on a particular area it is unique from the point of view that it fulfils his need to have long trains of coaches, and four can be operated at once, running impressively round the track. Trains also venture 'outside' into the sometimes inclement weather and reappear as if they have been on a distant East Coast Main Line journey.

In many ways, John's layout is built on firm foundations, as the baseboard framework and trackwork are all the work of accomplished track builder Norman Solomon. It's a relationship that both have enjoyed for over 25 years, Norman having been first involved in building trackwork for a 4mm layout of John's. This was at Great Budworth, then when John moved to Over Peover work began in a small way on a small O gauge stretch. Like myself, John has always been fascinated and a firm fan of O gauge. From there John's railway interest moved into the present shed but was only half the size it is now.

Bold decisions were then taken. In a conversation between John and Norman, John expressed a desire to extend the shed and enlarge the railway. Norman responded with the following words: 'Well none of us is getting any younger, so if we're going to do it, let's start now.' Much work was then undertaken by Norman and others building track, stations and a wide range of other features to arrive at the existing layout stretching in length to over 100 feet. A testament to Norman's skill is the layout wiring using yards and yards of multicoloured wires beneath the boards. This enables smooth running all over the track, bringing into operation motorised points and even signals that 'bounce' once they are cancelled.

John has always busied himself in all his various layouts in putting the finishing touches to buildings and

John Ryan and Pete Waterman.

scenery. Using a variety of tools and materials, he adds weathering, vegetation sprouting from building roofs, as well as meticulously arranging groups of figures in stations, goods yards, in signal boxes and at work on the line side.

I'm fascinated that the layout can be worked in two periods: the LNER in the 1930s, and British Railways during the 1950s. The 1930s were of course the halcyon years of the LNER with Nigel Gresley designing wonderful locomotives and carriage sets. John has a splendid array of both blue and silver A4s from this period and examples of the named trains: the 'Silver Jubilee'; the 'Coronation'; and the 'West Riding Limited.' This is besides over 60 Pullman carriages. John has subtly weathered some of the named carriage sets, seeking original photographs of the vehicles to help in giving them an authentic appearance.

An office within John's house is the hub of his business empire. Sitting incongruously amongst his various important documents, are batches of carriages and also wagons awaiting attention, when he can steal a few moments of his precious time to give them attention. In total he has approximately 300 carriages.

The 1950s period includes many ex-LNER Gresley A4 and A3 Pacifics. These are complemented by an impressive number of Peppercorn A1s and A2s.

John has applied fine detailing to both locomotives, carriages and wagons. Within the locomotives, all operated by DCC, John has asked Cliff Williams to cleverly add both sound and smoke to give further authenticity. Small lights within locomotive cabs replicate open fire boxes, lights illuminate in carriages, even for a short period when stopped in a station; and lamps also glow at the ends of guard's vans.

The track layout, locomotives and rolling stock, as in real life, require a fair amount of attention and John has a number of specialists who help him keep everything running smoothly.

I have looked for long periods at the great number of pin-sharp pictures in this book, so much so that I am easily transported back to my thoroughly enjoyable days on Leamington Spa Station. I do hope the book evokes similar favourite steam memories in other rail enthusiasts.

John with his present layout. Photograph by Cliff Williams.

CHAPTER ONE
BEGINNINGS

John Ryan was born in Doncaster, South Yorkshire, during May 1950 amidst a period that saw Britain gradually awaking from the nightmare of World War Two. Rationing of food and commodities was being relaxed, industries were nationalised to promote job security and the National Health Service and Welfare State had both been founded to improve the lives of millions of people. This new age was embodied in the Festival of Britain, which was launched in 1951 with the aim of celebrating British industry, the arts and sciences and inspiring the thought of a Britain that was recovering and moving forward into the future.

A similar feeling of optimism and drive towards improvement has been with John all his life. He has found success within the cosmetic surgery business, particularly with the Transform Medical Group and Make Yourself Amazing (MYA), and spearheaded the magnificent achievements of Doncaster Rovers, lifting the club out of the Conference League into the Championship, whilst fighting for a much-needed new stadium. Despite all this activity, John has managed to cultivate his other passion — model railways. Starting with a small set as a boy, he has managed to build several more over the years, culminating with the present Over Peover layout, which is one of the largest O gauge model railways in the country. Being very proud of his origins in Doncaster, John has taken inspiration for his rolling stock from the famous locomotives and carriages built at the town's world-renowned workshops.

Yet, Doncaster almost missed out on the railway altogether and the townsfolk have Edmund Beckett Denison to thank for the rich history and vital transport links it has provided for over 150 years.

During the 1840s the Great Northern Railway company's original plan for the London to York route avoided Doncaster and extended via Lincoln, Gainsborough and Selby. Denison (Doncaster's MP) and others were at pains to point out to the GNR that the natural route of the railway should run as near to the Great North Road as possible. Fortunately, Denison and Robert Baxter, a local solicitor and fellow campaigner, successfully persuaded the GNR Board to extend their railway line via Peterborough, Grantham, Retford and Doncaster. The town subsequently managed to retain the importance on the railway system it had always enjoyed on the highway. Denison commented: 'Had I not fought to bring hither the Great Northern Railway, the town would never have been known for anything but its market and races'.

Between 1848/9 the line was constructed and subsequently joined several other railway systems (Midland, North Eastern, Great Eastern, Lancashire & Yorkshire) giving Doncaster its unique share in a railway movement that changed transport methods of the whole nation.

During June 1851, Edmund Denison was successful in persuading the GNR Board to transfer their main locomotive repair works from Boston to Doncaster. The company eventually favoured Doncaster because of its close proximity to large coal fields and centres of iron founding in addition to good water communications. When the Works, or the Plant as it has since become known, was established in 1853 it covered an area of 11 acres. By the early 20th century several buildings had been added to enhance the important role played by the area in the GNR's locomotive, carriage and wagon production and repair. These included: Erecting Shop; Paint Shop; North Carriage Shed; Crimpsall Repair Shop; Weigh House. Wagon construction and repair was removed to a site south of Doncaster in the late 1880s.

House building for the expected influx of workers started immediately, with railway enclaves being established both in Doncaster itself and outlying districts, such as Hexthorpe and Hyde Park. Workers arrived from many areas of the country including Lincolnshire, Staffordshire and Derbyshire. As well as houses, other facilities such as churches, public houses and schools were built. By the end of the 19th century Doncaster's population had doubled.

At this time Doncaster Works' most famous product was Patrick Stirling's 4-2-2 express passenger engine. These locomotives, which raced the company's important expresses between King's Cross and Doncaster, became known as 'Eight-Footers' or 'Singles' because of their eight-foot driving wheels. These were later replaced by H.A. Ivatt's 4-4-2 'Atlantics'.

Herbert Nigel Gresley succeeded Ivatt in 1911 and would remain in overall charge of locomotive and carriage design and construction at Doncaster until his death in 1941. During this period Gresley would conceive some of the most widely known locomotives in Britain and the rest of the world.

Perhaps the most famous are his 4-6-2 'Pacific' designs. Gresley's first Pacific was no. 1470 *Great Northern* which emerged from Doncaster in 1922.

Initially, express locomotives were not required by the GNR due to the recent introduction of Ivatt's Atlantics, but during the First World War an increase in train weights necessitated a more powerful type. Gresley dwelt on the matter until a suitable design had been formulated and new components tested on other types then being introduced. The result was his A1 Class Pacific which appeared shortly before the GNR was amalgamated into the London & North Eastern

GNR carriages ('Sheffield Stock' open third no. 3047 is in the foreground) receive attention from craftsmen at Doncaster Works.

A1 Class Pacific no. 4472 **Flying Scotsman** *is seen in an official picture taken before being displayed at the British Empire Exhibition in 1924. Due to restricted space 4472 had a 6 wheel tender fitted for the exhibition held in 1925.*

A4 Pacific no. 2509 Silver Link *between duties in early 1936.*

Railway (LNER) in the Grouping of Railways in 1923.

The third A1 to be completed was no. 4472 *Flying Scotsman*, emerging from the Plant during 1923. No one at this time could have foreseen that it was destined to become one of the most famous steam locomotives in the world. The A1 Pacific was the subject of further tests and developments during the late 1920s and new engines built between 1928-1935 were reclassified A3. Those erected prior to this time received modifications and also became A3 class members.

Gresley's Pacific locomotive design reached its peak between 1935-1938. British railways companies had traditionally taken the approach of running expresses in a slow and steady manner. But following high-speed train services being brought before the public eye by the much-publicised 'Flying Hamburger' train in Germany and the Bugatti railcars in France, the LNER decided that similar services might be introduced between King's Cross and Newcastle. The locomotive designed by Gresley especially for this high-speed work was the A4 Class Pacific. Always at the forefront of new ideas, Gresley turned to streamlining in order to give the locomotives an edge over the close timings of the new service. The secondary effect of this gave the design a very unique appearance for a steam engine in Britain at the time and the A4 was quick to attract admirers for its appearance. All the locomotives in this class were Doncaster-built and the first one to emerge was no. 2509 *Silver Link* in September 1935. The engine duly went on to set the speed record for steam traction on the press demonstration run and then proved highly reliable in service, working the 'Silver Jubilee' for the first three weeks single-handedly. But the most noted 'Pacific' performance was achieved on July 3, 1938. No. 4468 *Mallard*, whilst hauling a 'test' train of 240 tons down Stoke bank reached a speed of 126 mph, thus attaining a record for steam traction that has not been beaten.

Running concurrently with the Pacific development throughout the LNER period was the construction of other Gresley classes of locomotives, like the B17, P2, V1, V2, K3, K4, N2 and J39.

After Gresley's death in 1941 he was succeeded as Chief Mechanical Engineer of the LNER by Edward Thompson. His period in office was limited in scope, since it mainly covered the war years when there was little opportunity for implementing new designs. Despite this, Thompson produced several classes including the B1, L1 and A2/3. None of the B1s were Plant-built but the prototype L1 and all the A2/3 locomotives were produced there.

Thompson retired in 1946 and was succeeded by Arthur Henry Peppercorn, the last person to hold the post of LNER Chief Mechanical Engineer. Peppercorn, in contrast to Thompson, was a great admirer of Gresley's ideas and reintroduced several of the latter's design characteristics. These appeared on his Class A2 locomotive built at Doncaster in 1947 and included cylinders being placed centrally above the bogie. A further 14 of these engines emerged in 1948. The A2 locomotives were successful, as were the new A1 Class Pacific, which had slightly larger driving wheels. The first batch of this type, however, did not appear until 1948 when all four main-line railway companies were merged in one national system.

Peppercorn retired in 1949 after producing only a small number of new locomotive classes. His A1 engine however was considered to be the most reliable 'Pacific' ever built at Doncaster and several former Plant employees recollect him saying he designed it, 'just how Gresley might have done had he lived longer.'

John Ryan has many models which reflect this golden era of locomotive construction at Doncaster. The same is true with his large number of carriages.

Carriage construction began at Doncaster sometime

after the mid-1850s, preceding that of locomotives by at least ten years. In 1876, E.F. Howlden was placed in charge of carriage matters for the GNR and he oversaw the design and construction of the company's stock, in addition to the East Coast Joint Stock, until 1905. During his tenure the Plant kept abreast of the large strides in carriage construction and passenger comfort which were taking place around the country. The first British restaurant car was produced at the works, along with the first side-corridor coach and another featured a steel underframe.

Nigel Gresley was appointed as Howlden's successor and he continued to improve the Doncaster product. His first designed train sets were built in 1906 for services between King's Cross, Manchester and Sheffield and featured Pullman vestibules and buckeye couplings. Gresley then went on to develop the bogies and introduce articulation to recycle outdated stock without resorting to costly replacements. Gresley held the post until stepping up to Locomotive Superintendent in 1911 and was succeeded by Edward Thompson, then later O.V.S. Bulleid, who immediately established a good working relationship with Gresley. A London-Leeds set, built in 1921, included a Kitchen Car, which for the first time in England contained electric cooking equipment.

Following Gresley's appointment in 1923 as Chief Mechanical Engineer of the newly formed LNER he moved from Doncaster to an office at King's Cross with Bulleid as his personal assistant. The two men along with other members of the Doncaster workforce formed a team to deal with all aspects concerning the LNER's locomotives carriages and wagons. After its initial conception at King's Cross, all new design work was carried out in the Plant drawing office, with small detailed designs being delegated to other LNER drawing offices.

The introduction in 1928 of the first non-stop 'Flying Scotsman' service was one of the great occasions in railway history. For the service, a new set of carriages was constructed and part of the Plant's work involved producing Restaurant Car triplets. Gresley took a personal interest in the vehicles' internal decor and asked his friend Sir Charles Allom, a furnishing specialist, to produce ideas for them.

The following decade marked a period of insecurity in the field of carriage construction since rail travel became increasingly threatened by the developments in road transport. LNER carriage construction actually

Interior view of the first class carriage in the 'Coronation' train.

ceased for a short time in 1932. But, despite this instability, the decade heralded Doncaster's finest achievements in carriage design.

In 1935 the Plant completed the 'Silver Jubilee' set for the high-speed King's Cross to Newcastle service and this was an immediate success with passengers. A pair of articulated twin carriages and a triplet restaurant set formed the train and these were constructed using standard teak frames, but with metal sheeting. The exterior panels were then covered in Rexine (an artificial leather) that was a distinctive silver/grey colour. The interior was suitably luxurious.

Two years later the Plant built the 'Coronation' train sets, introduced to coincide with the Coronation celebrations of King George VI. These hoped to emulate the success of the 'Silver Jubilee' on the London-Edinburgh express service. Construction was similar to the 'Silver Jubilee' but with the omission of Rexine and the colour scheme was changed to garter blue for the bottom half and marlborough blue for the upper portion. A distinctive feature of the set was the 'beaver-tail' observation car placed at the rear of the train and used in the summer months. Another group of carriages appearing in 1937 was the 'West Riding Limited' set, which operated on the Leeds-Bradford-King's Cross services.

At the time John Ryan was born in 1950 the Plant had fallen under the control of British Railways two years

The 'Coronation' train as completed at Doncaster Works in 1937.

earlier. R.A. Riddles was the Mechanical and Electrical Engineering member of the Railway Executive and his focus was standardising new locomotives and carriages. In the ensuing years the Plant would no longer turn out named Pacifics steam locomotives or anymore trains of great luxury like the carriage sets of the late 1930s. Instead, the Works largely focused its attention during the 1950s to building standard class steam locomotives and carriages to modest designs.

At the beginning of the 1950s approximately 4,000 workers were employed at the Plant. Besides being known as a railway town, Doncaster between the 1890s and mid-1920s had also developed as a coal mining centre with over a dozen collieries being established in former surrounding rural villages. Many thousands of workers were employed and large housing estates were established.

Two of John Ryan's uncles worked as fitters in the Plant but both his grandfathers were coal miners. His father, Oscar, worked at International Harvesters as a chief inspector. This was just one of the companies that were established in the former Wheatley Park area, north east of the town centre. Other companies which had taken root there, mainly in the 1930s when the Wheatley estate was broken up, included Pilkingtons, British Nylon Spinners and Crompton Parkinson.

Oscar took John to watch high-speed trains hurtling through the town's railway station around 1956. They both watched from the station's cattle dock, adjacent to platform 1 on the east side of the complex. At this time a common sight would be Gresley A3s and A4s,

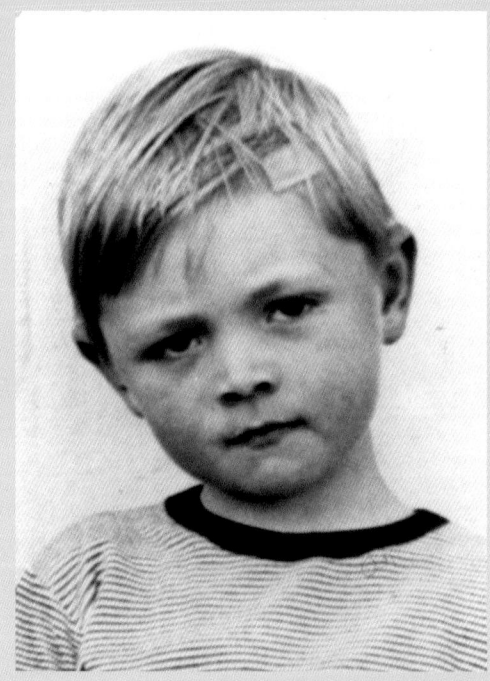

A youthful John Ryan.

as well as Peppercorn A1s, hauling such trains as the 'Elizabethan', 'Flying Scotsman' and the 'Queen of Scots'. The main line from King's Cross split three ways just north of Doncaster where express trains would continue to Edinburgh, Leeds or Hull. Secondary services headed by B1s and ex-GCR 'Directors' would travel west to Sheffield or Manchester and all places beyond. Coal traffic from the surrounding collieries would pass through the station as well as along the Avoiding Line a short distance to the north.

Standing on the Doncaster cattle dock, John Ryan's imagination was captured by the fantastic visual spectacle of huge, impressively powerful A4s racing by at great speed, rods thrashing and belching smoke or pausing briefly surrounded by steam in the busy railway station. These deep impressions have stayed with him ever since and inspired him to recreate these visual memories via his enormous model railway.

The 1950s are particularly significant to the development of John's model railway because the middle of the decade saw the publication of BR's Modernisation and Re-equipment Plan. This was a blue-print for an attempt to halt the losses being suffered by BR due to the competition for passengers and freight from private cars and haulage firms. Among the recommendations implemented were the replacement of all steam traction with diesel and electric.

The loss of steam was seen by many enthusiasts as a devastating blow, almost like a death in the family. Consequently, when building steam model railways, enthusiasts have tried to recall something of that unique feeling when they first watched with fascination a steam locomotive pass by — their layouts try to recapture those lost magical moments.

Although regretting it now, John did not venture to the Doncaster Carr Loco shed or Plant Works, though as he grew older he realised how important Doncaster was as a railway centre. He was always more captivated with operating a model railway.

Initially, during the early 19th century, the fascination with model railways had grown alongside the development of the railways themselves. Indeed it could be argued that models of locomotives existed prior to them being realised. Models or prototypes were often created before life-size locomotives, carriages and wagons were built.

Once the railway age had brought about massive social changes, expensive live model steam engines appeared for the wealthy enthusiast. Cheaper ones were made in a variety of sizes and materials (mostly wood, lead and tin) and were either crude pull-along engines or propelled by clockwork along a simple makeshift track.

Early toy trains were made mainly by German manufacturers based in or near Nuremberg. One of the earliest was Mattheus Hess, who built tin toy trains in the 1820s. By the 1880s, celebrated manufacturers, such as George Carette, S. Guenthermann and Theodore Märklin, had begun production.

Amongst the most celebrated was the Gebrüder Bing firm, which from the 1870s produced very high quality sets including minutely detailed stations. A model railways' landmark was reached during 1891 at the Leipzig Toy Fair when Märklin introduced a layout which could be put together piece by piece as well as added to. At the same time the company made available its 1-5 track gauges. A little later their O gauge track was marketed and this was the gauge (in name at least) that John Ryan would adopt to build his magnificent railway.

Märklin's engines were powered by clockwork and the main material used in assembling the bodies was painted and soldered tin plate. The products were sold in Britain, France and the US. By the dawn of the 20th century, electric-powered models had made an appearance on model rails.

Britain's own model railway industry started early in the Edwardian period with Wenmen Bassett-Lowke of Northampton, the son of a boilermaker and engineer. Already, Bassett-Lowke supplied engineering items to wealthy amateur model engineers constructing live steam locomotives. After a trip abroad aged 22, he realised he could make a vast profit importing German built locomotives that were adapted to resemble British engines and sell them to wealthy adult enthusiasts. These were not toys but elaborately detailed and impressively engineered models. This was a significant step forward in the history of British model railways. His first model was the *Black Prince* locomotive — over two feet long and costing in excess of £500 in today's money.

Between 1900 and 1914, railways in Britain were at their peak and this era has been called the golden age of railways. At this time there was a desire amongst wealthy men to have models of the cutting edge locomotives as well the carriages they hauled.

To help Bassett-Lowke with this venture he appointed Henry Greenly, a master of engineering design, who also founded the first magazine devoted to model railways. Builders of Bassett-Lowke's models included the German companies of Bing and Carette. A further development was for him to introduce locomotives that were large enough to haul wealthy owners and their chums round extensive gardens; some large engines also became a feature at seaside amusements.

Bassett-Lowke's High Holborn shop in the early 1900s.

Eventually Bassett-Lowke stores were established in Holborn, London, as well as Manchester and Northampton.

In the years leading up to the First World War, Bassett-Lowke's business boomed and model railways developed with various fusions of ideas taking place amongst the main companies, electricity becoming more widely employed.

As may have been predicted, German exports were severely restricted during the 1914-1918 war and Bassett-Lowke's profits plummeted and continued to do so for some time after the conflict ended. Many enthusiasts did not want to buy models made in Germany.

Undeterred, Bassett-Lowke moved production to a new British factory in Northampton and aimed scaled down models at a wider market beyond his former very rich clientele. Whilst these smaller models could be operated in smaller houses, the model railway pastime was still nonetheless for the affluent and brought Bassett-Lowke continuing success during the 1920s.

Competition for Bassett-Lowke in the UK model railway market came from Hornby trains run by Liverpool-born Frank Hornby. He was responsible for establishing Meccano in 1907 (at first titled Mechanics Made Easy), Dinky Toys and the launch of *The Meccano Magazine*.

According to Anthony McReavy in *The Toy Story* (2002), Hornby first entered the world of model trains at the Industries Trade Fair in 1915. Fortunately for British toy manufacturers, the War enabled them to fill the gaps left by the German rival companies. Hornby launched his first toy model railway train set in June 1920. These were toy railways aimed at middle-class children — not large course scale model railways — the market catering for adults by Bassett-Lowke. It is worth noting that while Bassett-Lowke did produce highly detailed models, these were largely for exhibition purposes, and were well beyond the reach of the ordinary family. The highly detailed A4s they produced in 1939 sold for £13/13/0 in both clockwork and electric, whereas the lesser detailed 4472 sold for £4/12/6 for clockwork and £5/3/6 for 8-10 volts D.C. electric. Both models were fitted with course scale wheels.

Hornby's train sets were immensely popular and a by-line used by the company at this time was 'British Toys for British Boys'. He targeted children using sophisticated advertising and branding techniques. Like Meccano, his train sets were meant to be expanded and developed, suiting a child's ambitions to create a railway world of their own.

From 1922 Hornby published annually a *Hornby Book of Trains* giving details of all the company's developments as well as what was happening on the railways. These enticed children into the model railway world, making them want to be part of it.

The 1920s saw the formation of four distinct railway companies in Britain. Some marvellously colourful liveries were used by the various express engines and exquisite carriage sets were produced to promote faster and more comfortable services. Impressive models of train sets from the four companies became available for enthusiasts. Sometimes these were endorsed by express train drivers who became part of the advertising campaigns.

By 1928, the first Hornby electric train was,

appropriately, a Metropolitan Railway electric. The set had electric lights, which could be switched on or off, on both the locomotive and train and were connected to a mains supply via an adaptor that plugged into a light socket.

At the end of the 1920s, the Hornby Railway Company was formed for enthusiasts and within a decade boasted 10,000 members with 400 branches worldwide.

In a number of adverts Hornby, now a household name, depicted both father and son involved with model railways, convincing people this was a good wholesome activity and something that should be greatly encouraged. Hornby provided a vast amount of model railway paraphernalia: signal boxes, stations, figures, animals, fences, milk churns, etc, in fact anything that could add reality and detail to the model railway landscape and ensure his modelling market was buoyant.

Shortly before the Second World War, Bassett-Lowke realised the model railway markets could be tapped even further if model railways were scaled down and prices were more attractive for the lower classes. Thus, he was instrumental in producing the Trix Twin 4mm brand in the mid-1930s which became amazingly popular.

Hornby in turn produced a rival scale — OO — and naming it appropriately Hornby Dublo; the locomotives powered by either clock-work or electric. By comparison with Trix, Hornby's goods were more realistic and more competitively priced.

A Trix layout exhibited in the late 1930s.

During the Second World War, Hornby turned to making munitions, model railway production not beginning again until the late 1940s. After the hostilities, railways and trainspotting became very popular with children and the Ian Allan Loco Spotters Club was formed around 1945 and quickly reached 80,000 members. Each year, with the co-operation of British Railways, they made organised trips in special trains along routes of interest.

Amongst the model railway developments in the early 1950s was the launch of Triang Rovex's model plastic train sets that were far more affordable to a wider market than hitherto. Some people argue that during the 1950s and 1960s model railways entered a golden age.

John Ryan possessed his first model railway at the age of five and it was laid out at Palington Grove, Cantley, a mainly working-class Doncaster suburb.

Perhaps a little surprisingly, given John Ryan's geographical connection with the old LNER area, this model railway was a Hornby Dublo three Rail *Duchess of Montrose* EDP 12 Train Box set. He subsequently became fascinated by aspects of the Great Central Railway after seeing Pete Denny's Buckingham Branch Railway in the model railway press as well as Portreath by David Essery. He had taken the *Railway Modeller* from 1960 and still has some of them as far back as 1962.

John's Hornby Dublo 'Duchess of Montrose' set.

CHAPTER ONE – BEGINNINGS 13

Boys playing with a Hornby set around 1948.

John attended Danum Grammar School, Doncaster where his favourite subjects were football and history. He regularly played as a striker in the school's football team and was a keen supporter of Doncaster Rovers. Hoping to take A level history and continue with the subject at university, he was forced to select maths, physics and chemistry instead because the school was 'technologically minded'. He never had any desire to leave school early and work on the railway or in the Doncaster Plant Works.

Progressing to Nottingham University, John studied Chemistry and during these years model railways took a back seat, though he did visit a number of model railway exhibitions to keep his enthusiasm alive.

Spending all his grant during the first few weeks of term at Nottingham, he sold encyclopedias part-time, regularly making ample cash for his efforts

'As far back as I can remember I always wanted to become a wealthy man,' John confessed. 'I don't know anybody else in my family who ever made any money. I believe I'm the first. I did not have a role model, yet I used to read books like *How to Become a Millionaire* and Dale Carnegie's *How to Win Friends and Influence People*.

Encyclopedias were the first items that he ever sold. Initially, he did not think selling was for him, though he knew he had a gift for it and, after two weeks, he was offered an area manager's job. He turned it down, saying he was a full-time student intent on becoming a forensic scientist. On leaving university in the early 1970s, John worked at Aldermaston Research Centre, under Professor Rutter, a leading forensic scientist, who had been involved in investigating the Moors Murders.

'Although I was in a very professional and interesting occupation, I was hard up because the pay was disgustingly bad. So, part time, I started selling central heating, earning about four times more each week than my other wage. Eventually, I said stuff having a career, deciding I would much rather work for myself'.

Consequently he began looking for further business opportunities to bring his ambitions to fruition; becoming a millionaire, turning Doncaster Rovers into a successful football club, and building an enormous model railway.

By the end of the 1970s, he was married with a young daughter, Claire, and living in Tickhill, Doncaster. His model railways interest returned and he began operating a small 4mm layout which was based on the Great Central Railway. A move to Cantley, another Doncaster suburb, saw him dedicate an entire bedroom to an ambitious 4mm model railway layout.

Engineers building locomotives from scratch (sometimes referred to as Scratch builders) have always existed from the early 19th century but model railways took a turn when commercial kit-builders entered the scene. In Robert Forsythe's *History of Locomotive Kits Volume 1* (1999) the author mentions that locomotive kits were in existence before the 1950s but when K's GWR 14XX 0-4-2T model appeared a milestone was reached. Thereafter, with other innovators making their mark 'the model railway kit was enabled to have an everyday role in the hobby'.

John met kit/scratch builder Bill Rodgers living in Handsworth, Sheffield, around 1982. He was fascinated when Bill showed him an O gauge locomotive moving along a short stretch of track. From that time John was convinced that O gauge was where he should develop his modelling interests. He also considered locomotives built from fine detailed kits (featuring effective photo-etching techniques introduced from the 1970s) would definitely be high on his dream layout once finances would allow. Kit manufacturers impressing John in the 1980s were Nu-Cast and DJH.

In 1978 John moved into cosmetic surgery with Transform, a Manchester-based company. Over the

Aerial view of John's Over Peover property. The railway shed is circled.

ensuing years he would, as chairman, build up the business and eventually sell it in a multi-million pound deal in November, 2002.

Moving to Great Budworth, Cheshire, in the mid-1980s with his wife and now two daughters, John dedicated another room to his model railway. The layout included a small O gauge test strip and the first O gauge locomotive acquired was an ex-GCR Robinson 11F 4-4-0 in BR livery — no. 62662 *Prince of Wales*.

John moved to a larger house in Over Peover in the mid-1990s. An entire barn-like building was dedicated to an impressive large 4mm layout, football and railway memorabilia.

Whilst business interests and model railways grew for John, he watched with massive disappointment Doncaster Rovers' fall from the Football League. In the late 1990s he became chairman of the club and put huge financial resources into the coffers which eventually greatly assisted them gaining League status once more.

The desire to move into O gauge also took control in the late 1990s. Within the 4mm layout John placed some O gauge track and slowly his stable of O gauge locomotives and appropriate carriages increased. Eventually, all the 4mm material was sold and finances ploughed back into O gauge models.

Having a great number of business interests John finds immersing himself in model railways helps him relax. 'A couple of hours will go by and I don't even notice. Model railways are a great de-stresser,' confessed John, adding: 'I like to do the scenery, weathering on the locomotives and lighting the buildings up.'

His main railway modelling interest is British Railways in the 1950s, but through reading books over the last 20 years has become absorbed by LNER locomotives and rolling stock from the 1930s. Examples in O gauge, from both periods, have been present for a number of years within his layout.

'If operating the 1930s period I put on Fred Astaire music. I cheat a bit when running in the 1950s as I play the Beatles from the early 1960s.'

John's first O gauge locomotive, D11 Class 4-4-0 no. 62662 **Prince of Wales.**

CHAPTER ONE – BEGINNINGS 15

CHAPTER TWO
LAYING TRACK

Norman making a rail at his home. Picture by T. Bagwell.

World-renowned trackbuilder Norman Solomon has been tasked with building several of John Ryan's model railways; a small one at Great Budworth, and the first and second large layouts at Over Peover.

Born in Essex during 1945, Norman is the son of a former Marconi employee who worked as an electrical engineer in the firm's Chelmsford factory. His family have no connection with railway employment, although Norman's father was interested in model railways and the young Norman followed in his footsteps.

'I have always been fascinated by model-making,' admitted Norman, 'and been a model-maker ever since I could hold a pair of scissors. I had a Hornby clockwork railway and would get bits at Christmas or whenever. We sometimes set it up along an alley-way at the side of our house and operated signals and other items.'

Norman has no engineering experience but has always shown interest in the subject. His dad was very practical and had one of the first electric drills. 'When I was about eight I stripped it down, cleaned it and put it back together again,' Norman explained.

Leaving school at 15, Norman served an apprenticeship in a small village bakery. When this finished, he then moved on to Joe Lyons' Cadby Hall complex. There, Norman was employed as a technician and was involved with processing and product development, which would influence his methods for railway construction through the use of set techniques and processes.

Norman left to run his own small bakery with a friend in Somerset during 1972. By this time he had constructed 'Ashmelton', which was one of the most impressive scenic N gauge railways in the country. 'In the same year I exhibited the layout at Central Hall Westminster,' said Norman, 'Sydney Pritchard of Peco came up to me and asked what I did for a living. I realised later he was tapping me up to see if I would work in the model railway world. When the guy he had subsequently hired left, I actually helped out making several models for the new "Pecorama". It made me realise I could work professionally in railway modelling.'

When the small Somerset bakery closed in the mid-1970s, Norman stayed in the area, retaining the building and using the space to build model railways for customers across the country.

Business has mainly come through personal recommendation. 'I've only placed three adverts in model railway magazines. That's all I've put out in my life,' said Norman. Railway modelling became a full time job around 1976/1977. 'Obviously, since then I've had high and low points.'

During his first years in business, Norman involved himself in many aspects of layout construction, including track and scenery. Because he earned an enviable reputation for track building he has done this more than anything else. Norman has never built locomotives from kits but has constructed wagons.

Those unfamiliar with hand-built track might ask why

A point under construction. Photograph by T. Bagwell.

this is necessary when branded track is readily available. Norman states simply that proprietary track is just not as good because the sleepers are too thick and can take months to successfully ballast. 'My track has a very thin sleeper that can be set and ballasted in one go. Some quite large sections of John's layout were laid and ballasted in about an hour, after the preparation was complete,' said Norman.

John adds: 'I never considered using branded track with any of my recent layouts. Norman, rightly so, has the reputation of being the best track builder in the world. I know several people with model railways that had the chance to use Norman but laid normal track instead and they have experienced running problems ever since!'

'My track works particularly well with John's layout,' said Norman, 'because it is very stable for trains running at high speed, which is what he wants'.

One of Norman's first big projects was the Lonsdale layout which was begun around 1979. It was featured in the first two issues of *Modeller's Backtrack* magazine in 1991.

'Lonsdale was based on a real location but with a fictitious track layout,' began Norman. 'All the trackwork had to be hand-built because plastic components were not available at the time and DJH supplied cast metal chairs for the rails. I worked on site in 10-day stints and it took about ten years to complete. I still visit the layout even today to carry out maintenance work.'

Norman first began to build for John Ryan in the mid-1990s when the Yorkshireman was living in Great Budworth, Cheshire.

John with his OO gauge layout under construction at Over Peover.

Norman and John with the OO gauge layout.

A3 no. 2752 **Spion Kop** *passes through Over Peover station on the first O gauge layout. Picture by Tony Wright.*

'The first item I built for John was a viaduct which has survived and is incorporated on the main layout today. Originally it had stretches of short track at either end for fiddling about with locomotives. That's when my work for him started. When he moved to Over Peover, I built, in the first building designated for a railway, a mixed layout. It included a 4mm railway and a short 7mm stretch with the viaduct.' When this building was required for other purposes in the early 2000s, a 10-metre square shed was erected down the garden to accommodate the OO and the O gauge sections.

Upon entering the shed, the O gauge layout was located on the left side and the OO gauge ran on the right. The two gauges were positioned at different heights, with the latter being lower down, this being necessary because of space considerations, which also forced both systems out of the building at each end. Trains were thus given maximum running time at speed and appeared as if they were on a journey. This has been an important requirement for the layouts in the shed and John particularly likes this aspect. Initially, the exterior track sections were exposed to the elements, but latterly a cover was added.

Both gauges had stations, scenic sections and storage lines. The O gauge station was named Over Peover and was quite modest with two platforms, a bay for branch trains and two through lines. There was a small goods yard and a one-road engine shed with large

D15 Class 4-4-0 no. 8800 approaches Norman's viaduct. Photograph by Tony Wright.

turntable. From the station the lines ran the length of the shed to tightly loop round outside to go through the middle of the shed on the scenic section, which incorporated Norman's viaduct. Exiting the building for the second time, the lines ran to a higher level behind Over Peover station and then went outside to come back in against the opposite wall where there were storage sidings. The final section of track took trains back outside and through Over Peover station.

The OO gauge was positioned in the middle of the room, with the O gauge scenic section adjacent at a slightly higher level. The smaller gauge allowed for a more extensive station — named Castle Cross, with eight platforms — set in the heart of a heavily industrialised city scene. Centrally-placed tunnels split the station from a large seven-road motive power depot with mechanical coaler and turntable.

The two gauges survived side-by-side until the late 2000s when John's semi-retirement allowed a concerted effort to be made on building up the O gauge layout.

Norman comments: 'John had spoken for some time about extending the original shed to bring the exterior tracks at the rear of the shed under cover and then expand the layout within the extra space. We were chatting in his office one day and I said that if he seriously intended to extend the shed he ought to do it before one of us dies. This was met with a lot of laughter, but before I left for home all the rear track had gone and the site was being prepared for the extension.'

John adds: 'I had always been impressed with O gauge. The size, weight of the stock and realism of movement just makes the whole experience that much more satisfying. I went up to Blackpool and swapped a lot of my OO gauge locomotives and carriages for O gauge stock. I also traded an N gauge layout I had for three O gauge locomotives.'

Three views of the OO gauge layout in the shed before removal, showing the station and the engine shed. All pictures by Tony Wright.

CHAPTER TWO – LAYING TRACK 19

'I knew what John wanted from the outset,' said Norman. 'It was a folded figure eight layout, not one where there was a lot of shunting. He wanted to show off long trains of both carriages and wagons, some of which he wanted to run at speed. The shed and layout have been enlarged several times, but basically, what we have now is a double track main line. Trains actually go round the room three times so you get a maximum viewing of them. There's not a lot of sidings and goods sheds which many people want to focus on with their layouts. There are no facilities for that in this case.'

'When the new shed went up I initially had a new 11 x 10 metre space, carpeted with lighting and an air-conditioning unit. By the time I went home after the first stint, John had trains running; albeit with temporary baseboards and track.'

When the shed was extended, some of the features of the O gauge layout existing were incorporated into the new plan, such as Over Peover station, and the viaduct. At first, an analogue 12V Kent Panel Controls system was used for operating the layout.

Initially, the first phase of construction did not include Castle Cross terminus station and the main running lines around the room were completed first. The terminus platforms and the very complex arrangement of lines for the station throat were built subsequently by Norman and transported from his home to Cheshire. Norman built the underframe from 4 x 2 soft wood and laid 12 mm plywood on top. He hasn't used anything else for the base because he argues it does not have the same integral strength. Some of the framework was built on site and also at his workshop. Sections built in Somerset were transported by van to Cheshire. He prefers to do this so he can be sure everything is level and square.

Norman says: 'To move the station boards in one piece, six of us manhandled lengths of 3"x2" into the basic position I wanted. I then got the legs and kicked them around until I had them exactly right. Until you get on site you're not 100% sure that things will work out the way you plan so some adjustments are necessary. All the connecting pieces that are critical to alignment were done in the shed.'

Progress is made erecting the baseboards in the extended section of the shed. All pictures by T. Bagwell.

The several stages of building Castle Cross station are seen here. The top left and middle images see the track and platforms fitted in Norman's workshop (photographs by Norman Solomon), whilst the remainder show the boards positioned in the shed (Pictures by T. Bagwell).

All the track is laid on a closed cell 3 mm polyurethane foam, which is supplied in 2 x 1 m sheets. 'I use that on all my layouts,' revealed Norman. 'John's layout has 3 mm foam even in the storage areas. To glue the foam to the board, and track to the foam, I use builders' PVA general adhesive made by Febond. I literally just brush it on.' Norman dislikes cork as moisture can cause it to expand and contract, whilst Febond is favoured over wood glue as the latter can become quite stiff and crack when dry, whereas the former is more flexible.

For the trackwork itself, Norman did not make many detailed plans as some builders might have done. 'John told me what he wanted and I roughly sketched it out. When I asked him if that was OK, more often than not, he said, "Yes, that's fine". From past experience he knew that I could successfully interpret the ideas in his head.'

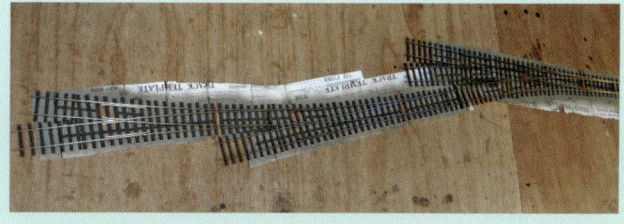

Points built on templates and ready for installation. Picture by Norman Solomon.

CHAPTER TWO – LAYING TRACK   21

'John's terminus has quite a complicated lump of point work. For this I worked out what I needed to achieve and sketched it out and then transferred that over to full-size templates just to make sure everything fitted in. Doing trackwork for so long, I can imagine for the most part what I want without spending time on detailed drawings. A rough sketch is usually all I'll prepare which is quite sufficient to work from.'

Norman used C&L templates for points as they spray bottle and some water-based acrylics.'

The sleepers and timbers are laser cut from plastic sheet to match the thin sleepered track. A wood grain is sanded on the top and they are cut to length and laid on the templates temporarily stuck in position by double-sided tape. C&L chairs are threaded on to the rail and are shaped with a sharp chisel to suit the location on the track. Norman then works from the stock rail to the opposite side bonding the chairs to the

The installation of the goods shed junction has been completed and Mike Sant takes a rubbing for Norman to build the points. Both pictures by Norman Solomon.

contained a lot of information which he needed when building. If they didn't provide the information he wanted he drew the arrangements himself.

When asked if there had been any difficult parts of the layout to complete, Norman was adamant that the work was all relatively straightforward. Yet, he did say that adding new points to the existing layout could offer challenges. 'You have to take a rubbing of the existing track and then build the point on that to know if it will fit. Most new sections are on a light curve and that had to be built into the point, but that is the kind of challenge I enjoy,' said Norman.

Norman's track bases are specially designed and manufactured by a firm in Essex. He can use up to a thousand metres of rail each year, along with many kilos of ballast. 'That's also made to my specifications,' offered Norman. 'The stuff you can buy is often the wrong size for the layout but mine is just right for O gauge. I've used between 20 and 30 kilos of ballast recently on John's layout.' Norman added: 'I've also got a special blend of paint to use on the trackwork. It's a grey/brown sleeper colour and I give the track a dusting before it gets laid. John likes to do a lot of the weathering as well and he'll do the detailing with a

sleepers and timbers with butanone solvent.

Norman has jigs, which are made from plastic, for soldering the vees used in crossings and this allows him to get the correct angle as there are many used in a typical layout.

Whilst templates are a helpful guide for Norman, he makes extensive use of a small mirror to check that rails are aligned properly and run through without any kinks. Gauges are also employed to check spacing, as is a bogie that has the wheels spaced at two extremes of the standard setting. A homemade gauge consisting of old sleepers is used to check the correct spacing between double track.

The only piece of rail Norman does not make himself is the switch blade, which he asserts are very hard to successfully produce by hand. Other rails are cut to the correct length and dressed using a file. A large coarse file is used initially to speed up the process, but a smaller finer one is used to finish the rail. A cheap vice is favoured as it opens up slightly when closed against a scrap piece of rail. The track being worked on is then easily inserted for filing. Norman is very particular about having three sets of rail cutters on him

Norman goes through various stages of laying track. All pictures by T. Bagwell.

at all times. 'With the amount of track I produce I can go through a pair of cutters in no time, so I always have two pairs spare and if I use one of these I immediately order another — I can't be without them.'

The layout is powered by one box so there is just one switch to use to power on or off. 'John's remit to me when we started was to keep things simple, so I have tried to follow that where possible,' said Norman, who has also wired the layout from the beginning, including all the new sections. The layout started out with an analogue system, but subsequently DCC has been laid on top, so now both can be used as all of John's locomotives have not yet been given the necessary upgrades. 'I've had to build four different panels as the layout increased in size,' admitted Norman, 'extra power supplies had to be included, to illuminate all the LEDs on the control panel as some had to be controlled by miniature relays which were taking the electricity.'

Every piece of track has a 0.6 polyurethane coated wire about 50mm long and stripped at each end as a dropper. One is soldered discreetly to the track and the other is bonded to a 16.2 multi-strand wire which goes back to the panel or point motor for switching. Several of the latter type are used to power various sections, being of different colours to categorise their use. All the inside rails are 'common' which are fed with the only black wire on the layout.

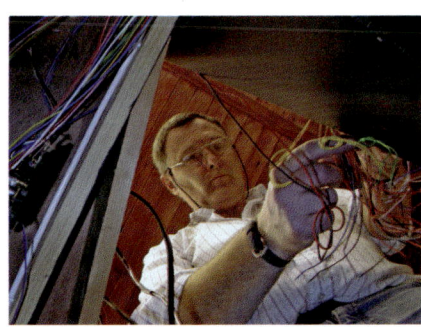

Electrical components installed by Norman: Fulgurex point motors: Castle Cross control panel. Top right picture by P. Tuffrey; others by T. Bagwell.

 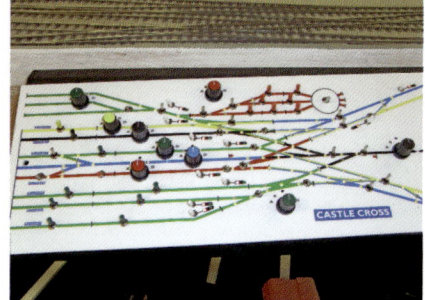 

CHAPTER TWO – LAYING TRACK

Smaller 7-strand wire is connected to the point motors and signals and these are also specific colours. Norman states that this is a must and makes life a lot easier when trying to find a fault.

Norman admits the wiring could have been arranged a little more neatly underneath the baseboards, but as there have been so many additions to the layout this has not been possible. 'There have been around 10 overlays to the control panel,' began Norman, 'but a problem with the wiring being too neat is it makes finding faults that bit more difficult. The wires have been loomed up and stapled to the baseboards just to keep them out of the way really.'

Norman has installed Fulgurex point motors across the layout and has been using these since he began working on the Lonsdale layout. 'All the point motors are Fulgurex — I've used about 2,000 during my career — and the majority are the original type not the newer ones, which I have found unreliable,' said Norman. 'Fulgurex point motors could be fixed in four positions and extended for use in tight places, but the newer motors have only two positions and can be problematic in areas with little space.' He added: 'The point motors have a 'suicide switch' that consists of a pair of diodes that work after the motor runs and reverses the polarity when the motor runs back again. In the stack with the suicide switch are subsidiary switches which can switch the point polarity and detect signals so that if the points are not set correctly you won't get the signal — it just won't work. In the station there is not much of this as it is too complicated.'

All points have switched crossings and do not rely on the blades to do the switching as there would have been far too many problems — only a small amount of dirt would stop the point from working so every crossing is switched from the point motor. There are gaps between the crossing and the blades (where the insulation is) and when the point changes the crossing switches polarity.

'For the station throat I worked out the details on a "crib" sheet to determine the necessary polarities and help organise the switching,' said Norman. 'The points are all numbered and relate to the point motor that switches it. This way you can wire a big chunk of the layout before going up top to check that you have got it right!'

The station throat is so complicated that certain points have to be in a set position for lines to work and these are marked on the control panel with black or red dots. 'Some pieces of rail have three or four electrical states and if they are left in the wrong one, they can cause confusion. It is a form of protection from incorrectly setting a route. The added complication is that the terminus is fed from two sides of a circle so you have polarity issues to contend with. These issues are sorted out automatically if the route is set correctly. There have been cries of "short circuit" when in fact the crossing has not been put back!' added Norman.

The control panel has been built with simplicity in mind. Norman commented: 'John's got the LED display so if he changes the points the route that lights up electrically sets itself for running. On other layouts I've seen, you have to set the points, then take several

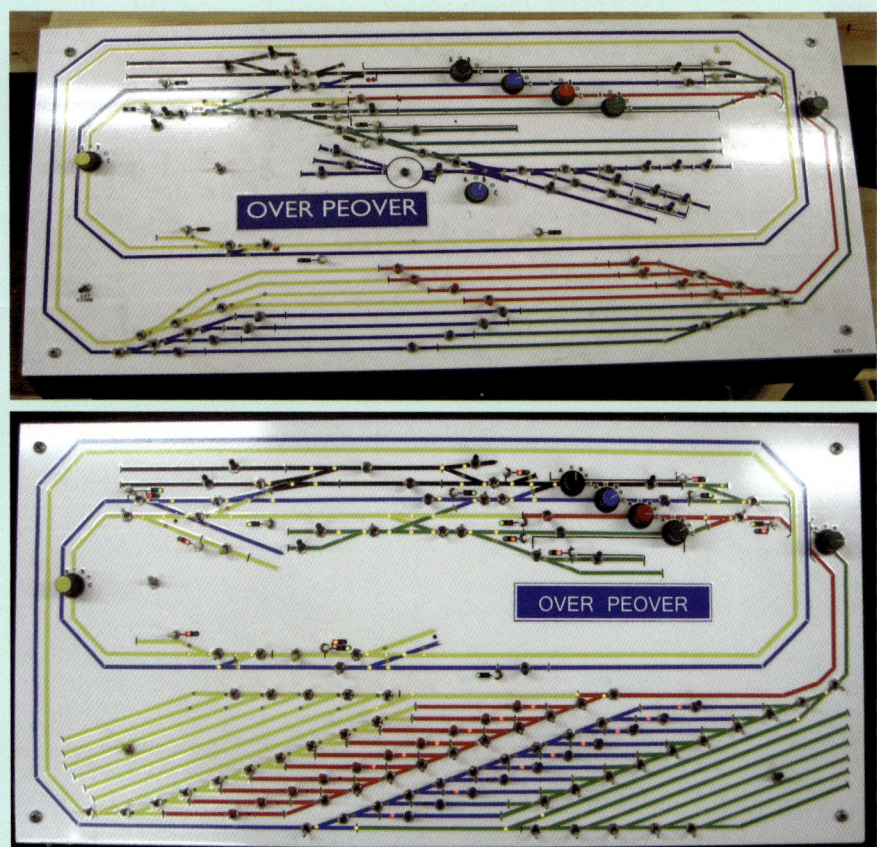

The control panel has evolved from that originally installed (top) to operate the various additions, including the goods yard, Castle Cross station and the storage sidings. Both pictures by T. Bagwell.

other steps for the train to run. The different colours on the control panel also represent a different wired section of track.'

The signals are operated by a servo control unit that is fed by a 12V supply. The negative supply goes through the switch and when the 0V signal is sent the signal operates gently. When the switch goes off the signal goes back with a bounce. In most cases the wire does not go straight to the signal, it goes through all the related points. If the switch is used and the points are set incorrectly, nothing will happen and the signal will stay on. The red light on the panel will go out and indicate there is a problem. 'This is a good failsafe for John,' commented Norman, 'as he is often running his trains at speed and goes back to his remit of operating being a simple process. All the thinking has gone into the wiring so the operator does not have to worry; if his route is set he has got it electrically.' There are a mixture of signals on the layout. Some were made early on by Tony Bagwell from parts from Scale Signal Supply, whilst later additions have been made by Karl Crowther; this is also true of the lighting posts.

The analogue DC controllers are made by All Components and are HH5 O Gauge feedback model. The DCC is an NCE Power Pro system, which has a central box that allows multiple controllers to be used. In this instance five Pro Cab models are employed and these can be positioned at several points across the layout for ease of operation, such as moving stock in the storage sidings which are located a good distance from the central operating area. Norman admits that this DCC controller was not his first choice, but he has since found that it is very user-friendly and 'people in the know' have said it is probably one of the best systems on the market.

The exterior track sections are laid on 12 mm plywood which in turn sits on treated wooden slats supported by fence posts concreted into the earth. C&L flexi track is used and has been pinned into position. This section of track is 'loose' jointed to allow for expansion and contraction in the weather. Multi-strand wire is again employed as the bonding wire because Norman has experienced fractures with single strand wire on other layouts due to the latter's inflexibility. 'You have to record the temperature when laying a section of track outside,' observed Norman, 'and then calculate an allowance for movement. In hot weather, or when the sun has been shining on the line, I've seen John's

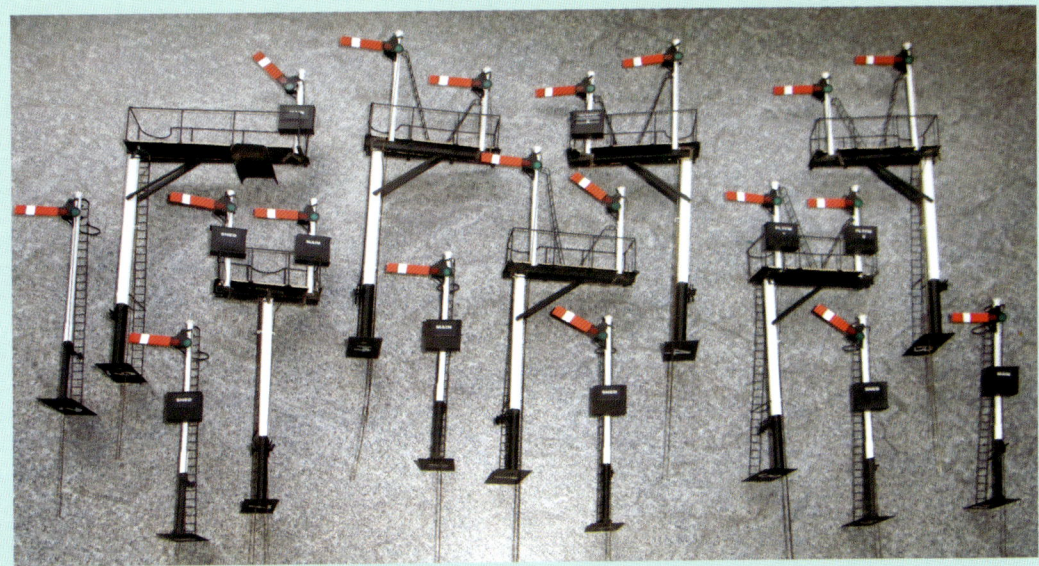

Hand-built signals for Castle Cross station. Photograph by T. Bagwell.

Norman works on the outside running lines. Picture by T. Bagwell.

Thompson A2/3 Class Pacific no. 60520 Owen Tudor *with an express on the outside running lines, which are yet to be covered over. Photograph by Tony Wright.*

track with no gaps between the rails when they had been 3mm apart previously. Originally, there was no cover over the outside running lines and they would get so hot sitting underneath the sun that you couldn't touch them or you would badly burn yourself.'

John's layout covers two periods: the 'golden age' of the LNER from around 1934 to 1939; the Eastern Region of BR during the 1950s. John explained that his interest in the latter had always been present as this was when he grew up, whilst the former had only really come to his attention in the last 20 years or so. 'The overlap is quite fortunate really,' began John, 'as not a lot changed with the buildings or the clothes people wore during that time — the figures particularly could belong to either period. The locomotives and carriages are also virtually the same but with a different livery so I only have to swap them to get the 'Coronation' or 'The Elizabethan' rather than

change the whole layout.'

Whilst many people with model railways choose to build with a particular place in mind, John has broken free of this restriction and has several scenes in which to view his locomotives running at speed with rakes of carriages or wagons. 'I like working on the layout, but the real enjoyment of it comes from seeing everything

Covers have been partially installed over the outside running lines. Picture by T. Bagwell.

working. There's nothing better than having *Silver Link* heading the 'Silver Jubilee' at speed towards Over Peover station with smoke bellowing from the chimney in sync with the movement of the connecting rods,' said John.

The shed is illuminated by fluorescent strip lights and circular LEDs above the layout. The main lights can be switched off and the LEDs then dimmed to the required amount in order to simulate anything between full daylight and dusk. All signals and buildings are illuminated, again with LEDs, to create a very atmospheric experience when the lights are dimmed.

Upon entering the building the first section on the left-hand side comprises the goods shed and wagon sidings that stretch approximately two-thirds of the length of the building. From the edge to the first roof support this part measures 88 in. by 37 in. and contains the goods shed, which has dimensions of 68 in. by 21 in. by 10½ in. There is a 4 in. gap between the wall and a large free area on the opposite side allowing vehicular access to the loading bays. The goods shed was made by Brian Lewis of 'Timber Tracks' and painted by Karl Crowther. Two lines enter the goods shed and run the length of the building to buffer stops at the other end. The tracks pass by two protuberances, with dimensions of 7½ in. long by 7¼ in. wide and 7¼ in. tall, that act as offices for the goods shed.

Interest is added to the scene through the addition of figures and lorries, including a W. Hodges van by Corgi (a replica of the one used in the popular TV series *Dad's Army*), one lettered 'British Road Services' (a Nationalised company formed through the Transport Act 1947, also by Corgi), a Scammell articulated lorry (Corgi), a Morris Traveller (by Lledo Vanguards) and an Austin 7 with Lipton's Tea livery (Oxford). All have been weathered by John. Grass has been added along the side of the building and on the opposite side of the roadway; fencing borders the whole section. The background of factories was also provided by Brian Lewis.

The first section of the goods yard (101 in.) contains

The following pictures tell their own story and are thus presented without words to accompany the main text.

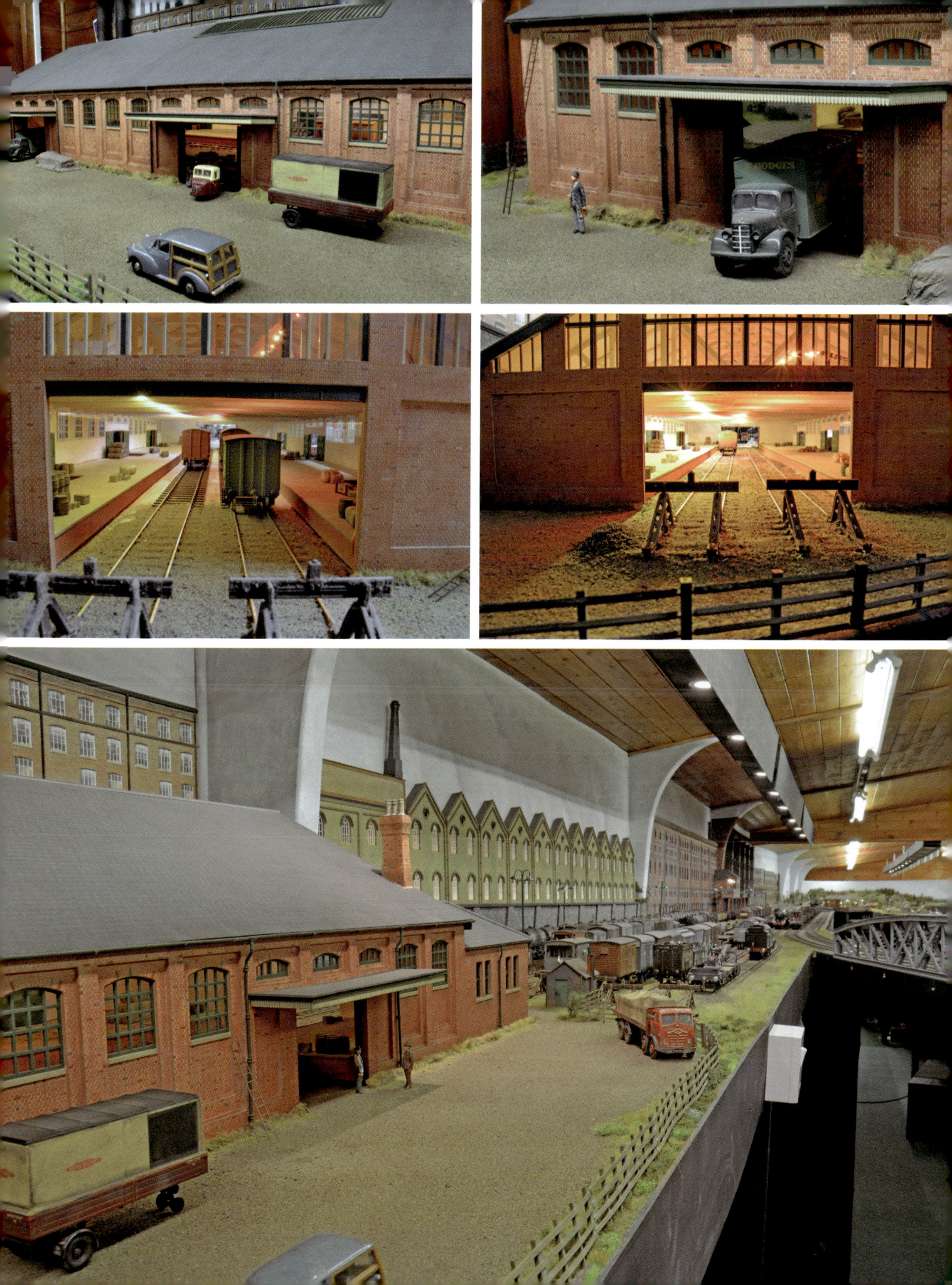

nine lines for storing the various goods and mineral train formations. A tall boundary wall stands on the left-hand side and above is a gabled factory backdrop from 'Timber Tracks'. The second section (101 in.) sees the number of lines reduced to eight as the far-right line merges into one on its left and a branch from the upper main line comes over from the right. An arched girder bridge carries these two lines and is 47 in. long by 32 in. wide, also being 5 in. high in the centre and 3 in. tall at the ends. This was supplied by Pete Waterman.

The impressive backdrop for this part of the goods yard is based on Huddersfield's London & North Western Railway and Lancashire & Yorkshire Railway goods warehouse, which has also been commissioned from 'Timber Tracks'. The building was erected in the mid-1880s and opened during July 1885, with the final cost being close to £100,000. Contemporary reports boasted that the warehouse was the largest in the country at the time and was also the most modern as the movement of goods across the different levels was given prime importance. The building was five storeys high with a basement and was designed in the Italianate style with red brick being used alongside blue brick for the details — windows, etc. A particular feature of the eastern side, which faced on to Huddersfield station, was a wagon lift of 30 tons capacity powered by hydraulics.

The adjoining backdrop depicts Manchester Deansgate goods warehouse, opened by the Great Northern Railway in the late 1890s. This was built in a similar style to Huddersfield goods warehouse, using red brick with blue brick details; the distinctive 'Great Northern Railway Company's

Goods Warehouse' was formed from white bricks and was present on all four sides. The side seen here is again the eastern face, but this did not face the railway and the bays opened to Watson Street for goods to be loaded on to carts. Manchester Deansgate was interesting because it provided facilities for the transfer of goods between the railway, canals and road.

The final 105 in. of the goods yard sees the eight siding lines converge into just two tracks that go on to join the main running lines. The lines from the end of the goods yard have a crossover allowing both tracks to be accessed. The scenery here changes to open countryside and this has been painted by Anthony Reeves of 'Treemendus'. A large signal box by Allan Downes sits at the end of the goods shed section where the lines meet the main lines running on the upper level.

The next section comprises a long, straight run through to Over Peover station, with connections to other parts of the layout. Starting from near the entrance to the shed, the first 52 in. — at which point there is a branch to the goods yard — has two sets of main lines. On the upper level are lines to/from the storage sidings on the opposite side of the shed, whilst those on the lower level connect to the scenic section, which stands adjacent to the storage sidings, and features a crossover. In between the two sets of lines are sidings. These two tracks immediately below the upper level are used for the stabling of goods trains and the three tracks raised slightly above the low level main line are for the storage of carriage stock. Perched above the tunnels outside are rows of houses purchased from 'Timber Tracks'. Telegraph poles line the upper level and these were produced by Tony Bagwell from castings belonging to Norman.

Further on, two tracks join the main line from the terminus station and the carriage sidings curve off to join that section. A signal box built by Allan Downes sits alongside the junction, where there is also access to the goods storage lines. The main line and goods sidings continue for approx 50 in. when they pass a small, one track engine shed built by John from a kit. In this section there are two short sidings and two longer lines running alongside the engine shed. Interest is added to this scene with a water crane and tower, two small buildings and figures.

Between the engine shed and Over Peover station there are several crossovers and a line to storage sidings hidden underneath the layout. This track passes underneath the high level running lines and goes past another Allan Downes signal box. The crossovers allow access to the storage lines alongside the engine shed, those running parallel to the upper level lines, the platforms of Over Peover station, the station branch platform and two short storage lines running along the edge of the layout.

The Over Peover section looking to the junction lines for Castle Cross station which are newly installed. Note the backing boards are still in place. Photograph by T. Bagwell.

The Castle Cross Junction lines as originally completed with boundary walls, since removed. Picture by T. Bagwell.

Installation of the small engine shed. Picture by T. Bagwell.

The two main lines run through Over Peover station, which is another product from Allan Downes, and alongside are the platform lines. These join the main line at the other end of the station and then go underneath the high level lines to the large storage sidings. John has created several interesting scenes on the station platform using figures (obtained from several sources), and the same is true at the station front. The vehicles parked at the station include an Austin 7 (Oxford), Jaguar SS100 (Solido), Bentley S1 (Verem), Austin 12 (Oxford), Morris Minor (Corgi) and an Austin FX3 (Ertl).

Standing above Over Peover station behind the high level running lines, are three groups of terraced houses from 'Timber Tracks'. On the corner of the first street is The Dyer's Arms pub and the final house on the second row is Ryan's corner shop, whilst the third street is completely residential. The first and third rows are the same length at 2 ft and the

centre group measures 14½ in. long; the street is 14 in. wide. The second and third groups feature house-side advertisements for 'Bovril' and 'Beecham's Pills' respectively and these would have been a familiar sight on similar properties during the mid-1930 to late 1950 period.

At the end of Over Peover station the platform lines merge with the main lines, which then curve round under the large flyover bridge from section one. The surrounding area is decidedly rural with farm animals, a small pond and rural dwellings in the background.

Castle Cross Junction and large engine shed sections under construction, late 2010. Photograph by T. Bagwell.

The third part of the layout includes the two engine sheds, castle and Castle Cross station. The northernmost part of the depot area was a relatively recent addition and originally the area ended near the turntable. The open ended six-track stone engine shed (12¼ in. deep, 25¼ in. wide, 7½ in. high) was built and installed by Norman. All six lines lead from the shed to the turntable, whilst a further set of two tracks run beside this giving access to the large mechanical coaler. This was obtained from Peter Smith of Kirtley Models, as were the office buildings spread alongside this part of the section, the small coaler and the large engine shed. The latter is placed 51 in. from the tunnels leading to Castle Cross station and measures 48 in. long by 16½ in. wide and 9¼ in. tall. There are four tracks running through the building, which is open at each end, and inspection pits are present at the tunnel end. Detailing in this section includes mounds of ash representing the waste removed from a locomotive's smokebox, discarded lengths of rails and sleepers and coal spilled from the tenders of engines using the mechanical coalers.

Originally the lines to the engine shed section were split from the lines out of the station to the Over Peover section by high retaining walls, but these have been removed to allow greater freedom of movement, especially to the carriage sidings stretching to section two. Looking to the station, the left tunnel gives access to the Over Peover section, the central tunnel leads to the engine shed, but there are also crossovers for the carriage storage sidings. The right tunnel provides contact with the scenic section. The tunnels burrow under a ruined castle built by 'Treemendus' and a short road. An interesting scene has been set up by John on the castle side with a figure perched on the tunnel parapet watching the comings and goings at the station. Vehicles featured on the road include a Bentley Mk VI (Lansdowne Models) and a Morris Oxford Traveller (Corgi).

Several views of the large depot and the addition of the small engine shed. All images by T. Bagwell.

The layout in April 2012 with several sections still to be added. Photograph by T. Bagwell.

The whole Castle Cross station section covers an area of 30 ft by 6 ft, with 24 ft being the length of the station and the station throat covering the final 6 ft. As stated previously, Norman built the platforms and trackwork, whilst the station was produced by Brian Lewis ('Timber Tracks') using laser-cut pieces; the building itself is 157 in. long by 114 in. wide. There are a total of eight platforms (running from no. 1-8 from left to right, as viewed from the castle), with a goods platform on the far left with carriage sidings, as well as there being another pair on the opposite side. The goods platform is a recent addition to the station and adds further interest to the station scene, which is liberally decorated with figures from various sources. These range from groups of passengers seemingly engrossed in conversation to those admiring the locomotives, or one that is checking the timetable attached to a roof support. Station staff can also be seen lineside and on the signalbox gantry. In addition to the timetable, there are numerous contemporary posters attached to the arched roof supports running the length of the station. Castle Cross signal box, which bears a strong resemblance to King's Cross signal box, was commissioned from Peter Smith (Kirtley Models). Also inspired by King's Cross is the small locomotive yard with turntable in the top corner of the station throat near the castle.

Photograph by T. Bagwell.

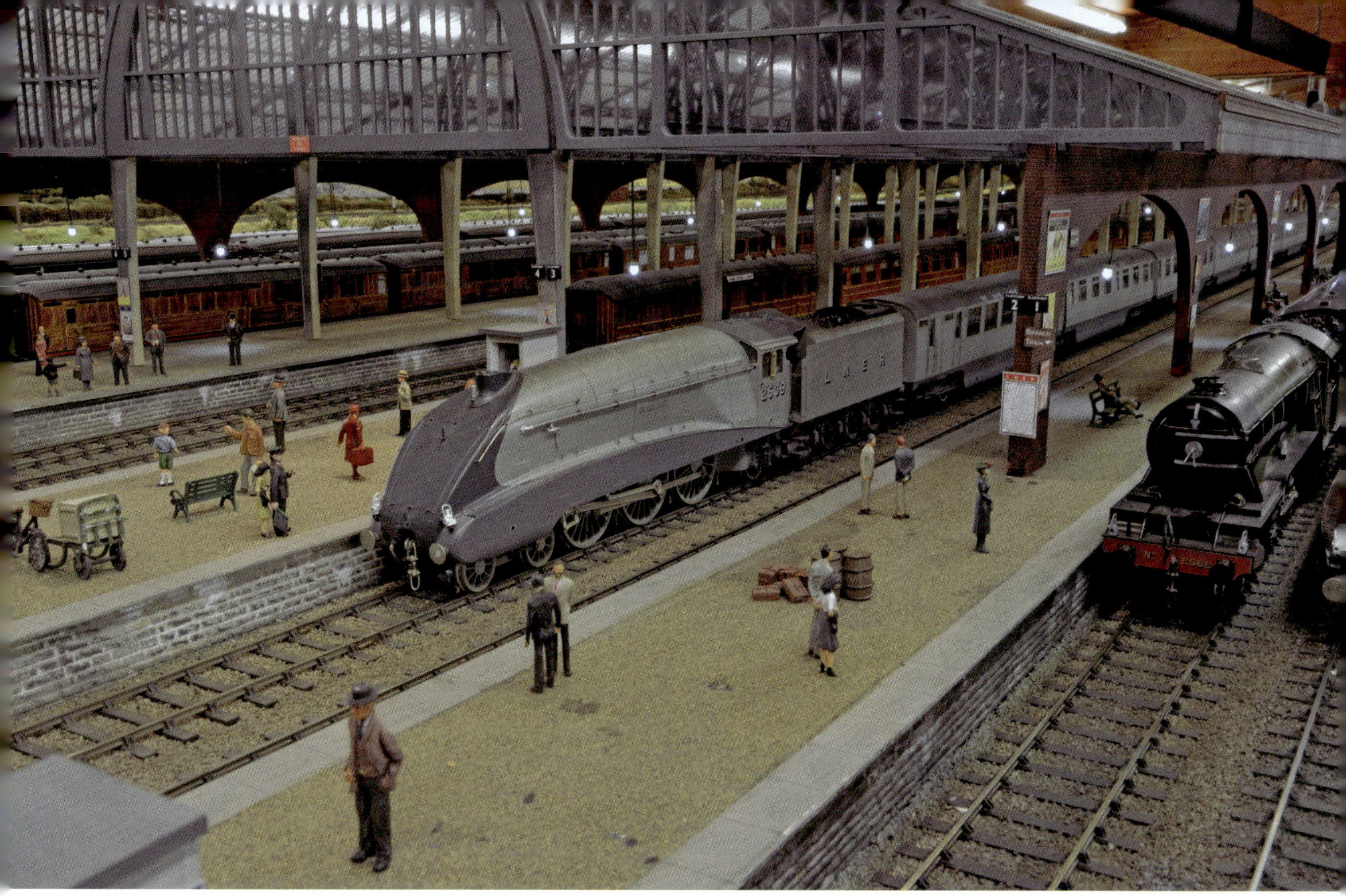

L N E R

L.N.E.R
BRIDLINGTON
BRILLO
soap pads
Shines Aluminum Fast
LONDON & NORTH EASTERN
CUNARD
L.N.E.R.
HELENSBURGH

3401
L N E R

L N E R

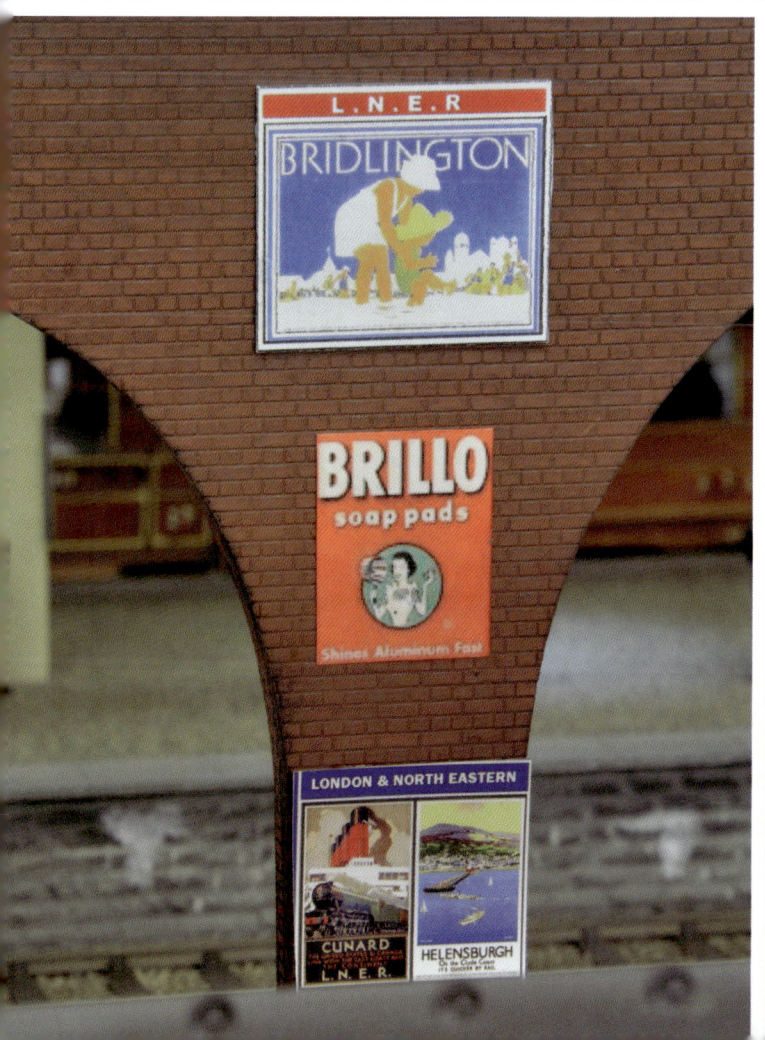

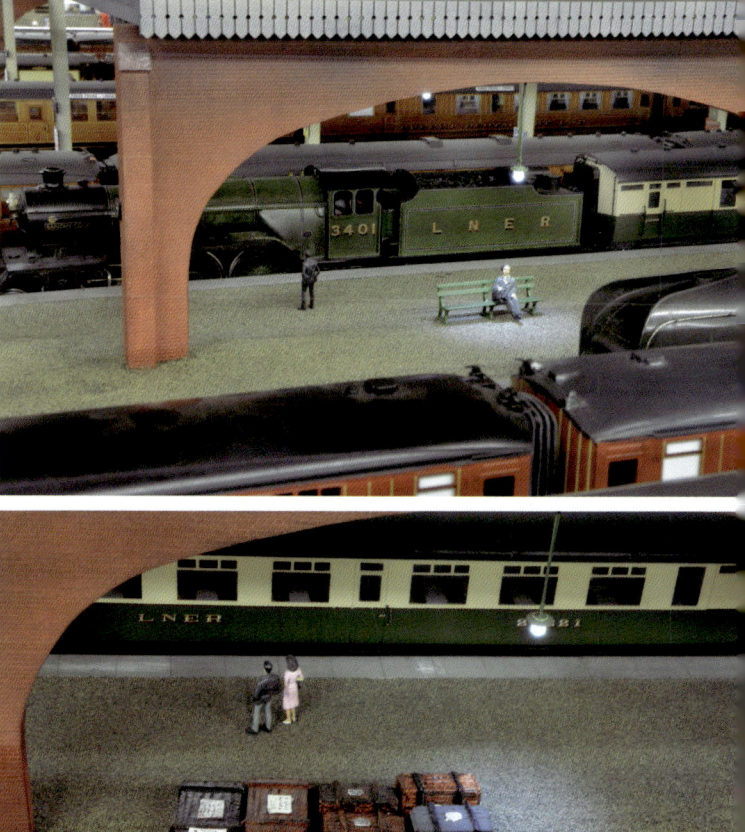

The scenic section starts with a tunnel for the lines leading to/from the lower level of Over Peover section. The backscene above the tunnel was created by 'Treemendus' (an interesting detail is the bird of prey in flight), as were many of the trees seen along the section and others on the layout. The two main running lines are flanked by a siding which joins them at the signal box (built by Norman). A short distance further on is the viaduct, with a total length of 47½ in. comprising three spans 8½in. wide, which was first commissioned from Norman in the mid-1990s.

Cattle can be seen grazing near the lineside at the end of the viaduct just before the main line sweeps off to Castle Cross station. Around 100 in. from the junction a small road bridge (built by John from a kit) passes over the main line, which then continues to the end of the building, curving round to the upper level lines on the Over Peover section. A goods loop parallels the main line at this point of the scenic section to just before the line begins to curve round. Interestingly, there were originally backdrops attached to the baseboards of the scenic section, hiding the area behind, which was later used for the storage sidings. These were removed, along with the same feature on the Over Peover section, to open the layout up and give increased visibility to the storage sidings and goods shed when they were installed.

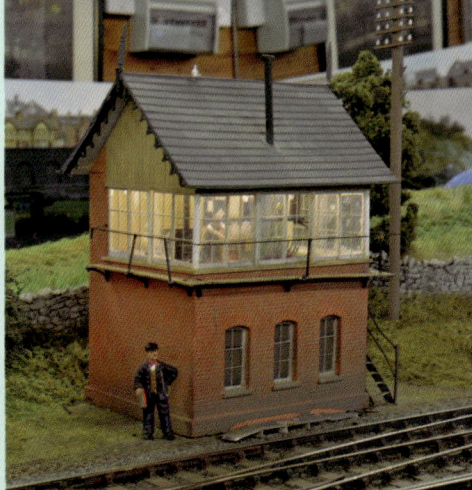

The scenic section under construction before the loop was added. Photograph by T. Bagwell.

The junction between the scenic section and Castle Cross station is laid. Picture by T. Bagwell.

The storage sidings span the entire length of the shed and the area is 34 in. wide, yet the volume of stock to represent two eras will not fit in them. Therefore, another set of sidings have been installed underneath — principally to house the vehicles not being run at the time — and accessed from the outside running lines. The top sidings are split into four sections, with the main line weaving in between them. There is a small city scene backdrop at the top end with a signal box and a railway bridge running across six sidings. These are split from the next sidings by the main line and the second set consists of ten lines, followed by another group of ten before the other main line splits the last six tracks. The backdrop for the three sidings is hilly countryside.

The storage siding boards, which were prepared at Norman's workshop, are seen in position in the shed and then assembled before the backing scene was added. Photographs by T. Bagwell.

CHAPTER THREE
LOCOMOTIVES

Modelling to encompass two eras — the LNER from about 1935 to 1939 and the Eastern Region of BR from 1948 to the late 1950s — has allowed John to accumulate over 150 locomotives. Many of these are based on the designs of Sir Nigel Gresley, but some from the constituents of the LNER are included in the collection as are some of Gresley's successors' locomotives.

There are many examples from Golden Age Models, L.H. Loveless & Co. and DJH, with smaller numbers from Connoisseur Models, David Andrews, FineScaleBrass, Rising Star Kits, Ace Products, Gladiator Models, Martin Finney, Eric Walford, Piercy and Tower Brass. Most have been bought new and 'ready to run', but some have been built specifically for John from kits, whilst others have been bought second hand.

In the main the locomotives are 'historically accurate' but in some instances there are errors. John appreciates that some modellers strive for exactness on their layouts and understands that this is perhaps where their enjoyment is mainly achieved. He hopes that the reader will appreciate his pleasure comes from seeing the locomotives moving at speed around the layout and will forgive any deviations from what would be considered '100% correct' for the model in a given period.

The main change carried out to any locomotive that John purchases is the fitting of new sound and smoke systems which is performed by Cliff Williams. He uses specially created sound clips from preserved locomotives, such as A4 *Sir Nigel Gresley*, A3 *Flying Scotsman* and new-build A1 *Tornado*, and loads them on to ESU sound chips. There are several sounds that are used: drive, whistle, safety valves, injectors, drain cocks, coal shovelling and buffering/coupling. For other classes of locomotive a 'generic' sound has been created. The chips work in conjunction with ESU smoke units which allows synchronisation according to the speed of the engine. The ESU smoke units are too large to fit in smaller locomotives and Seuthe units are installed instead. No one brand of speaker is used as the sound can vary between applications.

The following chapter has been split into two sections to show the locomotives as they would run on the layout in the LNER and BR eras.

LOCOMOTIVES IN LNER ERA

GRESLEY A1/A3 PACIFICS

Although introduced in 1922 by the Great Northern Railway, Gresley's A1/A3 Pacific design is undoubtedly associated with the LNER. The class distinguished themselves on the company's expresses, particularly the 'Flying Scotsman' of the late 1920s and early 1930s when running non-stop over the nearly 400-mile course. In the run-up to the introduction of the A4 Class, no. 4472 *Flying Scotsman* achieved the first official recording of 100 mph with a steam locomotive and this was followed soon after by a high of 108 mph from no. 2750 *Papyrus*.

The class were somewhat downgraded in importance after the introduction of the A4s, but were still a valuable asset to the LNER and were put to work on trains such as the 'Yorkshire Pullman' and 'Queen of Scots Pullman'. Several were also transferred on to the ex-Great Central Railway section to work expresses from London Marylebone to Manchester.

Generally speaking, there were few readily noticeable changes to the A1s/A3s during the pre-war years. The early tender with coal rails was the original Great Northern design. The later high sided LNER tenders were either non-corridor, or corridor for the King's Cross-Edinburgh 'non-stops' to allow the crews to walk through from the first carriage to relieve the original footplate crew. Other noticeable changes from A1 to A3 included conversion from right to left hand drive, and lowering cab roofs/chimneys and domes to meet the reduced height of the LNER loading gauge, as the original A1s had been built to the generous GNR gauge. The livery of apple green with black and white lining was standard. Lettering was in gold with red shading to the right and black below, and a white broken separating line. John's A1/A3 collection is just weighted more towards the LNER period. The locomotives have either been erected from kits supplied by DJH or purchased from L.H. Loveless & Co.

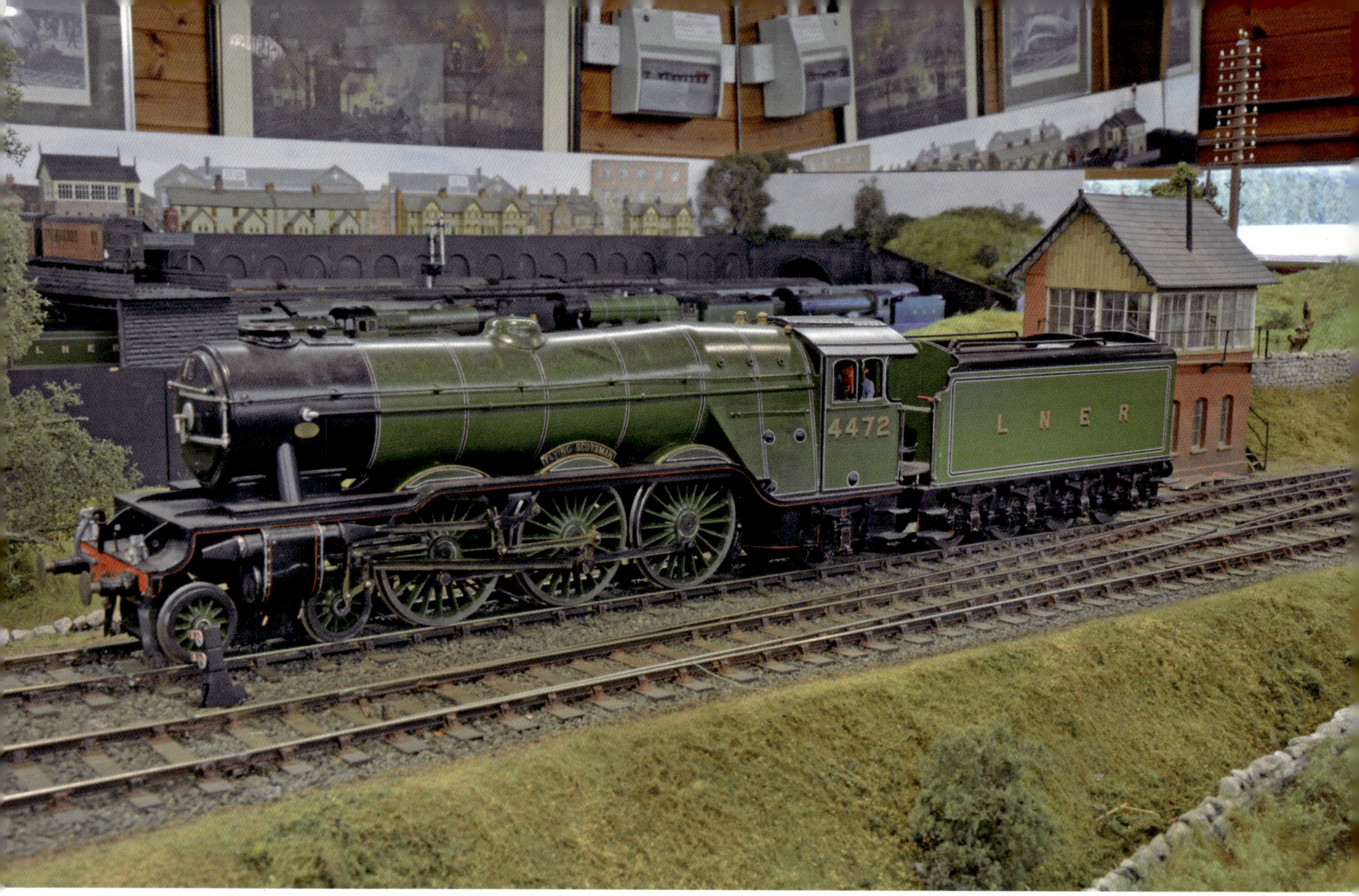

4472
L N E R
FLYING SCOTSMAN

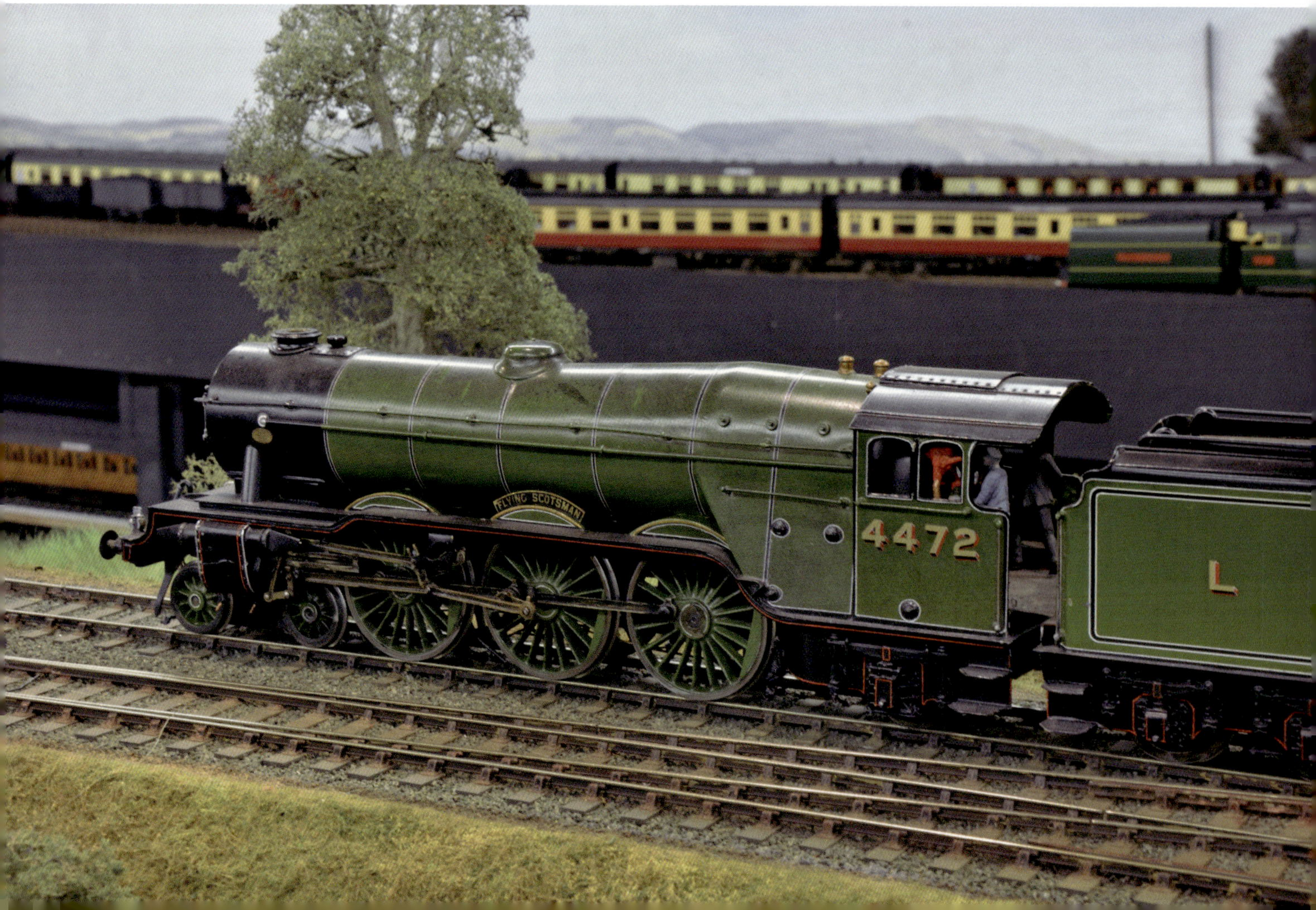

FLYING SCOTSMAN
4472
L

4474 VICTOR WILD

LNER 4474

THE SILVER JUBILEE
NEWCASTLE AND LONDON IN 4 HOURS

LNER 4474

GRESLEY A4 PACIFICS

Arguably, few other locomotive classes have captured the public's imagination than Gresley's A4s. From their introduction in 1935 the class have made headlines in both the railway and national press, gaining legions of fans in the process. John is one such follower and the A4s form the greatest part of his collection of locomotives.

Following the disappointment of P2 no. 2001's performance in service and in France on test, Gresley abandoned plans to continue with the unorthodox features of that engine and reverted to A3 specifications for his new A4 design. However, the boiler pressure was increased to 250 lb per sq. in. to give greater reserves of power and particular attention was paid to the steam passages, which were polished to reduce pressure losses from friction and the piston valve diameter was increased from 8 in. of the A3 to 9 in.

One of the most distinguishing features of the A4s was the streamlined exterior. The use of this feature for railway purposes was a relatively new science, but Gresley was quick to recognise the sound scientific arguments for the benefits that could be achieved. The shape of the new locomotive was determined in a wind tunnel and was expected to reduce wind resistance, therefore bringing about a saving in fuel. Whilst there were definite practical benefits to streamlining the A4s, the feature helped to promote the LNER through publicity, which was the main reason behind other railway applications of streamlining during the same period.

In the event streamlining only formed one of several reasons for newspapers and magazines to report on the A4s. On the press demonstration run during September 1935 no. 2509 *Silver Link* — decorated in a noteworthy livery of a silver grey with battleship grey and black highlights — reached a top speed of 112½ mph near Arlesey and achieved the speed record for steam traction. As no other A4s were ready at the time, no. 2509 worked both 'Silver Jubilee' trains daily for three weeks without respite to a very high standard of punctuality.

The dual successes of the A4s and 'Silver Jubilee' service ensured that more locomotives and new high speed trains were introduced by the LNER. Seventeen A4s were ordered from Doncaster to be used on ordinary expresses, but in the event five of these went on to be specially chosen to work the 'Coronation' high-speed service from King's Cross to Edinburgh scheduled to start in early July 1937. Nos 4488-4492 were named after dominions of the British Empire and given a special colour scheme of Garter Blue with red and white lining, with the front and frames being black. In addition, another two were chosen from this batch to be used for the 'West Riding Limited' which departed from King's Cross to Leeds and began in late 1937.

Another attempt was made at the speed record on the press run of the 'Coronation', but this came to naught and left the LNER in the shadow of the London Midland & Scottish Railway which had claimed the honour the previous day while demonstrating their own 'Coronation Scot' service. On its trial run on 29 June 1937 the 'Coronation Scot' reached a record speed of 114 m.p.h.

Following the completion of the order for 17 A4s, Doncaster Works progressed on to a request for a further 14 and these were in traffic for mid-1938. Four of this number were fitted with Kylchap blastpipes and double chimneys, which served to improve the efficiency of exhausting smoke and steam into the atmosphere. This efficiency of the Kylchap double blastpipe also reduced coal and water consumption.

One of these engines was no. 4468 *Mallard* and the locomotive was selected to take part in brake tests during early July 1938. In reality this was cover for an attempt to take the world speed record for steam traction. On July 3, 1938 with Driver Duddington at the controls and Fireman Bray with the shovel, *Mallard* was pressed to 126 mph just north of Essendine on the run down Stoke bank to Peterborough, thus achieving the world speed record for steam locomotives that is still to be surpassed.

When war broke out in late 1939 the A4s were immediately put into store, but soon afterwards returned to traffic to meet the growing needs of a nation at war. With the high-speed expresses discontinued for the duration and the number of services reduced, heavier trains abounded, but the A4s rose to the challenge with ample reserves of power. However, the class did suffer from reliability issues due to the skilled labour shortages caused by the conflict.

The first four A4 Pacifics were given the silver grey

livery, but thereafter a return was made to the LNER's apple green for a time. Initially, this followed the same design as the 'silver engines', but doubts were expressed as to whether the paint would stand up to the heat near the smokebox and on five engines the black applied to the front was extended to the first boiler band. The five 'Coronation' engines then emerged into traffic wearing Garter Blue and this was subsequently accepted as the standard for all members of the class and remained so — apart from during the war when black was applied — until mid-1949.

Golden Age Models has been the main supplier of John's A4s, both in LNER and BR livery and these have been constructed using brass. Interesting points of these models include an accessible smokebox and detailed cab interior, which in many cases has been embellished by John with figures of footplatemen. Recently John has added an LED to the firehole door area of several locomotives (including some A4s) to simulate the glow of the fire for when running in low light situations. The model of no. 2509 *Silver Link* was obtained from L.H. Loveless & Co.

GRESLEY B17 4-6-0

The ex-Great Eastern Railway lines in East Anglia presented problems to locomotive engineers as there were a number of severe weight restrictions in place. With the traffic generally heavy because of the boat trains to Harwich, there was difficulty in providing sufficient power within the required axle loadings. After struggles at both King's Cross and Doncaster Drawing Offices, the task was passed on to the North British Locomotive Company, yet in the event the company was also unable to fill the remit and only built 10 B17 locomotives.

Further examples were erected at Darlington and Robert Stephenson & Co. up to 1937 when a total of 73 were in service. Although mainly populating the GE Area, a number of B17s also worked on the GC Area; all were employed on express services or secondary passenger through to the 1950s when replaced on many trains by B1s.

GRESLEY P2 2-8-2

The P2s were initially conceived to handle heavy holiday traffic on the notoriously difficult line between Edinburgh and Aberdeen in the early 1930s. In the planning stages, Gresley decided that the first two members of the class would differ considerably in order to evaluate several features that had been gestating on a number of locomotives across the LNER fleet.

The first P2, no. 2001 *Cock o' the North*, was fitted with Lentz rotary cam operated poppet valves, ACFI feedwater heater and Kylchap double blastpipe and chimney. Following on was no. 2002 *Earl Marischal* which was equipped with standard Walschaerts/Gresley motion working piston valves and exhaust steam injector, but did receive the Kylchap arrangement.

No. 2001 was met with great ceremony when completed at Doncaster in May 1934. At the time the engine was the largest to be built in Britain for passenger service and similarly pioneered the use of eight coupled wheels for the duty. The press immediately claimed this behemoth was the most powerful passenger engine in the country and the fact was subsequently established on a press run in mid-June. *Cock o' the North* was running up the 1 in 178 gradient to Stoke summit with 649 tons (18 carriages plus dynamometer car) when a reading of 2,090 drawbar horsepower was achieved at just over 57 mph. Such a figure were unheard of in Britain at the time.

No. 2001 worked during the summer in Scotland and was found to be highly capable if also flawed in several areas. No. 2002 entered service later in the year and was not dispatched to Scotland until mid-1935, along with no. 2001 which had been tested in France during the winter. No. 2002 was considered the least troublesome and the engine's specifications were used for the four class members that subsequently entered traffic in 1936.

Earl Marischal did suffer one problem which needed to be rectified, namely that of smoke drifting to the cab and obscuring the visibility ahead. This resulted in a second pair of deflectors being fitted in 1935 and was partially the reason for the adoption of the streamlined front end on nos 2003-2006 and later *Cock o' the North* and *Earl Marischal*.

John has both no. 2001 and no. 2002 in his collection and both have been purchased from L.H. Loveless & Co. *Cock o' the North* is in original condition with LNER apple green livery and lining, whilst *Earl Marischal* is modelled on the locomotive when rebuilt with streamlining in late 1936.

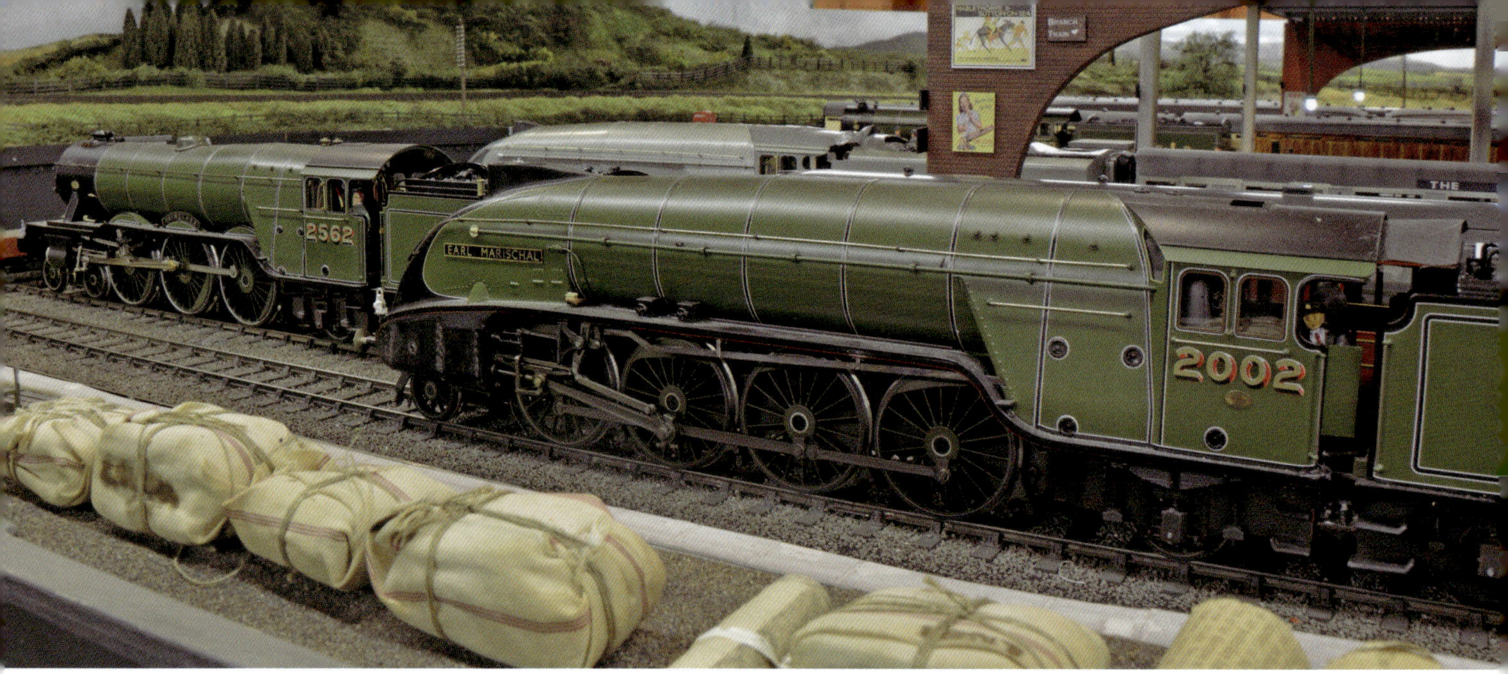
2562
EARL MARISCHAL
2002

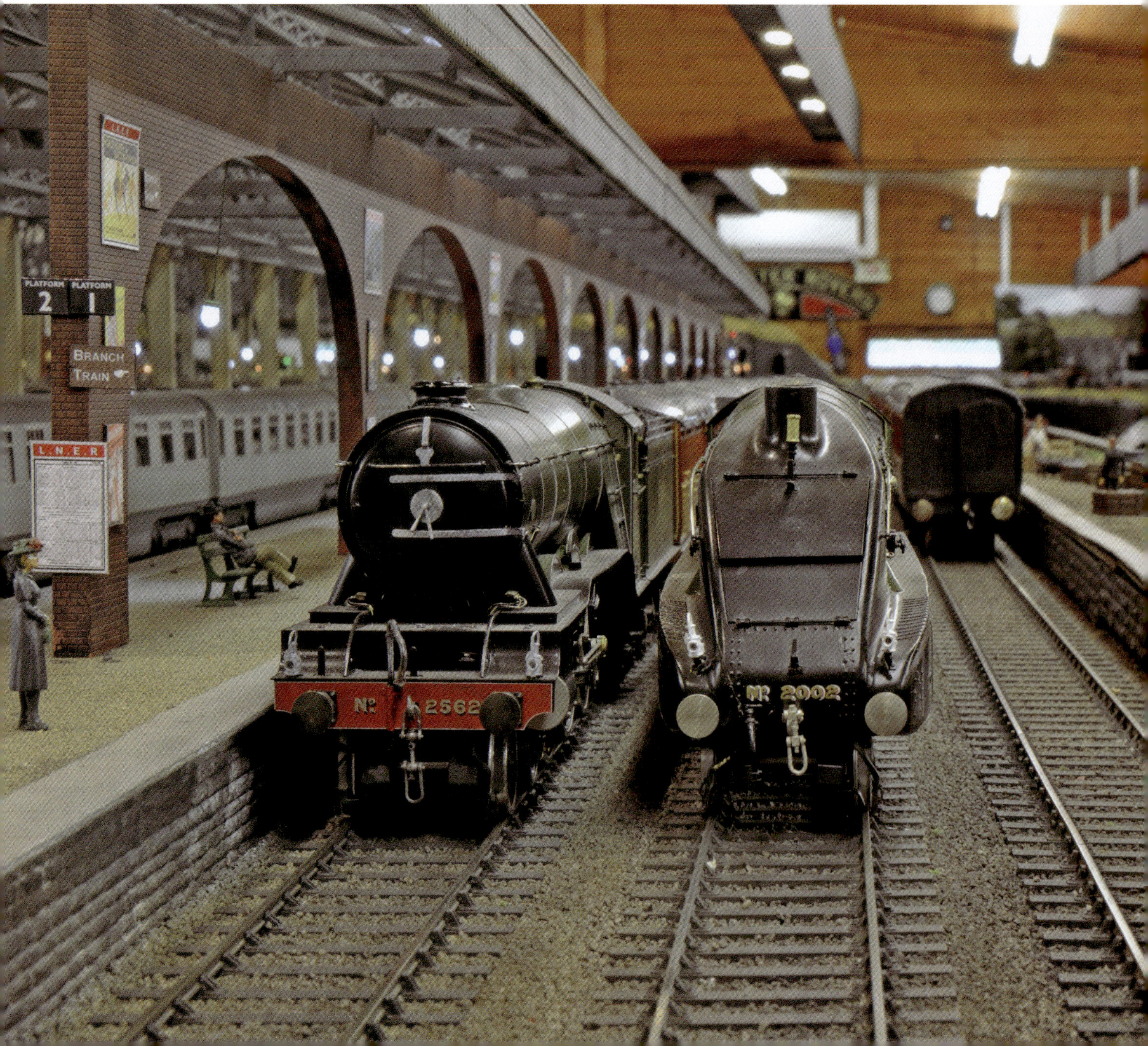
PLATFORM 2
PLATFORM 1
BRANCH TRAIN
L.N.E.R
Nº 2562
Nº 2002

GRESLEY V2 2-6-2

Following on from the P2s and A4s was the V2 2-6-2 design. Introduced in 1936, the class was mainly intended for fast freight trains, but as the design shared a similar boiler to the A4s the V2s were equal to any passenger train under both the LNER and BR. Of the 184 eventually erected only 25 were produced at Doncaster, with the remainder being completed at Darlington.

As the engines entered traffic they were sent to principal depots along the main line, being concentrated at King's Cross, Peterborough, Doncaster, York, Heaton, Edinburgh St Margaret's, Dundee and Aberdeen. Other sheds had only a few locomotives on the roster.

The V2s were all sent into traffic wearing apple green livery with lining and remained so decorated until the war.

No. 4780 has been purchased from FineScaleBrass.

GRESLEY W1 4-6-4

Before P2 no. 2001 *Cock o' the North* was built and embodied Gresley's desire to improve efficiency, W1 no. 10000 carried this mantle. Built in 1929, the locomotive had been in the planning stages for several years. This was due to the inclusion of a feature that was highly unusual for railway purposes. No. 10000 was to be fitted with a water-tube boiler that was set to work at very high pressure. Initially, this was to be 350 lb per sq. in., but was later increased to 450 lb per sq. in. Gresley hoped that the use of such high pressure would achieve a good saving of fuel.

No. 10000 was extensively tested before finally entering traffic, causing a great stir in the process with a highly unconventional shape due to the design of the boiler; the battleship grey colour also set the engine apart. Working from Gateshead shed, no. 10000 was a capable locomotive, being used on several named and important expresses, including the non-stop 'Flying Scotsman'. Yet, the uniqueness of the design contributed to several weaknesses and ultimately caused the project to fail. The locomotive was taken to Doncaster in 1936 and emerged the following year with the appearance of an A4.

John's model of no. 10000 was obtained from L.H. Loveless & Co.

OTHER LOCOMOTIVES

B3 CLASS 4-6-0

Introduced by J.G. Robinson for the GCR in 1917, the 9P Class 4-6-0 improved on his previous design by employing four cylinders instead of two. Only one 9P was built before a further five appeared from Gorton in 1920, with no. 6168 (then no. 1168) *Lord Stuart of Wortley* being the final class member. The class were considered difficult to work, resulting in high fuel consumption, and were used at Immingham until they were tried on the GN main line, working from King's Cross and Copley Hill (Leeds) sheds. Not living up to expectations there either, the class moved back to the GC lines, settling at Neasden where they worked trains between London, Leicester, Nottingham and Sheffield. Gresley subsequently rebuilt all class members with Caprotti valves. No. 6168 has been built from a David Andrews kit and is modelled on original condition with LNER apple green livery and lining.

B4 CLASS 4-6-0

The GCR 8F (LNER B4) 4-6-0s were designed at the turn of the century for fast freight and fish trains, but were no strangers to passenger services owing to their 6 ft 7 in. diameter wheels, which were unusually large for their intended use. A total of ten were erected by Beyer Peacock & Co. in 1906, with no. 1490, as GCR no. 1095, being the first to enter service. The locomotive worked across the GCR system for over 30 years and was the first class withdrawal in 1939 but was reinstated due to the war. A further five years were then spent in service. Wearing wartime black livery and the first Thompson number, no. 1490 was created from a Gladiator kit.

B16 CLASS 4-6-0

Produced from the end of the First World War until Grouping, the NER S3 Class (LNER B16) 4-6-0s numbered some 70 examples. The locomotives were primarily used on fast freight trains, but were also stand-ins on expresses, especially summer excursions. From new the engines were equipped with self-trimming tenders capable of carrying 5 tons 10 cwt of coal and 4,125 gallons of water. No. 2365, which has been constructed from a kit, entered service in December 1922 and completed nearly 39 years in traffic before condemned. The engine is modelled with LNER plain black livery with no lining; for the NER lining would have been applied.

B19 CLASS 4-6-0

Unfortunately, the GCR I Class 4-6-0s (subsequently LNER B2 before reclassification to B19) were one of Robinson's poorer designs. This was due to several shortcomings concerning the two inside cylinders and firebox. After starting service on the principal GCR expresses, the class were relegated to freight duties for a time before moving a step up to secondary passenger trains which they remained on until condemned in the late 1940s. From introduction to the early 1930s, the engines were based in Manchester, but were later divided between Sheffield and Immingham. Locomotive no. 5426 *City of Chester* was built in 1913 and withdrawn in 1944.

C2 CLASS 4-4-2

Patrick Stirling's 'Singles' became internationally famous through their exploits on the GNR main line. However, by the time H.A. Ivatt took over in 1896 the class were becoming unable to meet the traffic requirements and a new express type was planned. No. 990 *Henry Oakley* appeared in 1898 and was the first British locomotive to use the 4-4-2 'Atlantic' wheel arrangement. The locomotive was generally larger than the 'Singles' and was capable of handling the main line expresses of the day. A total of 22 were completed at Doncaster before Ivatt incorporated a larger boiler with a wide firebox into the design and a further 94 were erected until 1910. Classified 'C1' by the GNR, the two types became unofficially known as 'Small' and 'Large' Atlantics. No. 990, which was subsequently preserved, is an L.H. Loveless & Co. model.

C4 CLASS 4-4-2

Initially, only two of Robinson's 8B Class (LNER C4) Atlantics were built as trials were to be conducted against 4-6-0s to determine which had superiority. In the event the Atlantics took the advantage and a further 25 were erected by the NBLC and Gorton between 1904 and 1906. The class worked the primary expresses of the GCR and GC Area under the LNER until the mid-1930s and then secondary trains through the war years until the engines were condemned. No. 2918 was the first of the Gorton batch completed in February 1906 and was the last class member to be withdrawn in December 1950.

D49 CLASS 4-4-0

In the mid-1920s, Gresley designed a three-cylinder 4-4-0 for secondary passenger work in the North East and Scotland. A total of 28 with piston valves were built before the end of the decade as Gresley then decided to experiment with poppet valves. No. 2753 *Cheshire* was part of the last batch with piston valves and was the first of these engines completed at Darlington in February 1929.

F1 CLASS 2-4-2T

In the late 1880s, the Manchester, Sheffield & Lincolnshire Railway (later GCR) required new locomotives to work the company's suburban services around Manchester. Parker produced the Class 3 2-4-2 design in 1899 and a total of 39 were built to 1893; no. 7099 appeared in February 1891. For over forty years the class remained on the same duty until replaced by modern engines, but no. 7099 managed to survive until January 1949 as one of the last class withdrawals.

F4/F5 CLASS 2-4-2T

The Great Eastern Railway built the most 2-4-2T engines out of the constituents of the LNER. The M15 design originated at the time of T.W. Worsdell and was built between 1884 and 1887 before being discontinued with a total of 40 class members. S.D. Holden resurrected the design in 1903 and a steady stream left Stratford Works up to 1909 when 120 had been added to the original number: all were used on GER suburban traffic, mainly in London. Holden later replaced the boilers of 30 with a type working at increased pressure; 180 lb per sq. in. compared to 160 lb per sq. in. originally, which resulted in the LNER providing two classifications at Grouping F5 and F4 respectively. No. 7236 has been constructed from a Gladiator Kit.

J39 CLASS 0-6-0

Gresley's largest class was the J39 0-6-0, with numbers reaching 289 by 1941 when production ceased. Darlington built the vast majority of these engines which were used in the main for goods services across the LNER system, although use on local passenger trains was quite common. The J39s were mainly free from modification during their time in service but variations between tender type existed. John's four J39s (one has recently been renumbered to fit into the LNER period) have group standard 3,500 gallon tenders with the vacuum reservoir mounted at the rear.

J50 CLASS 0-6-0T

Designed by Gresley specifically for the hills of West Yorkshire, the GNR J23 Class 0-6-0T was introduced in 1914. After Grouping, the decision was taken to make the design a group standard class — J50 — and 38 were built at Doncaster between 1926 and 1930; a final batch of 14 were erected at Gorton between 1938/1939. The class mainly resided at either Leeds or Bradford, but other areas received examples for various periods; a quantity were used in Edinburgh for a number of years. Shunting and local freight duties were the mainstay of the class workload. Interestingly, John's J50s are all from the '583' series, which incorporated all the group standard features, and three of the four have numbers from engines built between March and September 1926. No. 610 has been built from a Connoisseur Models Kit.

K3 CLASS 2-6-0

With the success of Gresley's motion for operating three cylinders, new GNR express goods locomotives were designed to feature the equipment along with a larger boiler. Ten H4 Class 2-6-0s were erected in 1920 and 1921, then after Grouping the design was chosen to be a Group Standard class and a further 183 (with some modifications) were completed from 1924 to 1937 and classified K3. The locomotives were generally used on freight trains, especially expresses, across the LNER system, but use on passenger services (mainly excursions) did occur.

N2 CLASS 0-6-2T

Following the First World War, Gresley produced plans for an upgraded 0-6-2T from Ivatt's N1 produced between 1907 and 1912. The new engines were to have a superheated boiler, piston valves supplying steam to larger cylinders and a greater water capacity. The North British Locomotive Company were engaged to produce the majority of the class and sent 50 to the GNR between

December 1920 and April 1921. The company used the engines on the London suburban services, as did the LNER until the late 1920s when they started to distribute locomotives across the system, but mainly to Scotland. No. 4726 has been completed from a Rising Star Kit.

O2 CLASS 2-8-0

Gresley's second design for the GNR was the O1 Class 2-8-0 which was used for the heavy freight traffic on the main line. He subsequently decided to develop the use of three cylinders instead of two and used the O1 as a base, resulting in the O2 Class prototype — no. 461 built at Doncaster in May 1918. Gresley was pleased with the results and more engines (25) were ordered between 1920 and 1923. Further locomotives would have been built, but large numbers of ex-Railway Operating Division 2-8-0s, which had been completed to a Robinson design during the First World War, were purchased as surplus instead. Small batches of O2s were completed during the 1930s and early 1940s, slightly increasing the class total.

O4 CLASS 2-8-0

Introduced in 1911 for heavy mineral traffic, Robinson's 8K Class 2-8-0 numbered 126 examples by the time the design was chosen as the standard engine to be used by the Railway Operating Division of the Royal Engineers during the First World War. A total of 521 were built and many were subsequently purchased by the LNER. No. 6316 was one such locomotive, being erected by Robert Stephenson & Co. in January 1919 and taken into LNER stock during April 1924. The locomotive has been built from a David Andrews kit.

V1/V3 CLASS 2-6-2T

The 2-6-2T wheel arrangement was overlooked by the constituents of the LNER. Gresley decided to use the formation for his V1 design produced in the late 1920s for local passenger work in Scotland, with later examples employed in the North East and East Anglia. A subsequent alteration to the design was the use of a boiler with higher pressure, with these engines classified V3; ten new engines were built, whilst some of the V1s were converted. No. 472 was built at Doncaster in November 1938 and altered in March 1943. The engine has been modelled from a Connoisseur kit. No. 7684 distinguished itself from the rest of the class by being the only one to be decorated in LNER apple green livery, which occurred in September 1946.

V4 CLASS 2-6-2

Just before his death in 1941, Gresley saw his final design enter traffic. This was the V4 Class 2-6-2 which was intended to be used in a mixed traffic role and have a wide route availability — 5,000 of the 6,500 (approx.) operated by the LNER. Only two were completed before Thompson discontinued the project in favour of his B1 4-6-0. No. 3401 *Bantam Cock* appeared in February 1941 and no. 3402 was completed in March. After trials in Scotland and in the GE Area no. 3401 was sent to Glasgow Eastfield and was used on the West Highland Line, later being joined by no. 3402. Both would remain employed in this manner until condemned in 1957.

'MERCHANT NAVY' CLASS 4-6-2

Although John is a self-confessed LNER enthusiast, a Bulleid 'Merchant Navy' Pacific has been admitted to his collection with the excuse that 'it is working a special!' Of course, O.V.S. Bulleid was also a former LNER man and was trained and worked at Doncaster Works before Grouping. He was then Gresley's second-in-command during the glory years and went on to be appointed CME of the Southern Railway in late 1937. Bulleid's first major design was the 'Merchant Navy' Pacifics, which incorporated many innovative features for the time. No. 21C1 *Channel Packet* was the first class member to enter service in June 1941.

LOCOMOTIVES IN BR ERA

PEPPERCORN A1 PACIFICS

For the final 15 years or so of steam running on and off the East Coast Main Line, the Peppercorn A1 Class Pacifics gave excellent service on several named trains, along with a number of other expresses. All the main depots with express passenger duties had several at one time or another and were recognised by drivers and firemen as free steamers and highly capable, if a little unsteady at high speed or after running high mileages. The A1s amassed many hundreds of thousands of miles during their short lifespan and are perhaps considered slightly more robust than Gresley's Pacifics.

Naturally, a number have been obtained by John for working his many expresses. All are the product of Golden Age Models and all are in BR green livery, whilst most have the early BR emblem on the tender. The locomotives are constructed from brass and use Faulhaber motors. In addition to performing the weathering process, John has added embellishments such as standard headlamps, headboards and figures in the cab.

THOMPSON/PEPPERCORN A2s

Thompson added to the LNER's Pacific fleet early in his tenure with the rebuilding of Gresley's six P2 Class 2-8-2s as prototypes for a new class. The result was a group of ungainly 6 ft 2 in. Pacifics that had chassis problems at the front end. Later classified A2/2, the group — infamous for their rebuilding rather than their capabilities — were reduced to working slow passenger and freight duties from York and Peterborough sheds during the BR period. The production engines (A2/3) performed slightly better but still had the weakness at the front end. This was eliminated by Peppercorn with his A2 design, although some class members had the steaming capacity reduced by the fitting of single chimneys. The A2/3s worked from Edinburgh Haymarket, York, New England, Gateshead and Heaton in the 1950s.

Both pictures by Tony Wright.

GRESLEY A3

All A1/A3 locomotives returned to LNER green after the war, and subsequently blue under BR, with first 'British Railways' lettering on the tender before the emblem was used. From 1951 a change was made to BR green livery with orange and black lining and still with the emblem, but later a crest was adopted.

The main change carried out to the class during the 1950s was the provision of Kylchap double blastpipes and chimneys which improved performance and reduced boiler maintenance. However, this did bring about the adoption of German-style smoke deflectors because of the softer exhaust associated with the Kylchap arrangement.

Although still in the shadow of the A4s, and arguably the Peppercorn A1 Pacifics, the A3s were still highly capable during the final years of their lives and worked some of the Eastern Region's long-distance expresses.

GRESLEY A4 PACIFICS

Despite victory in 1945, the country was slow to recover and the railways were particularly affected through overwork and lack of maintenance during the war years. Named trains were gradually reintroduced and the 'Flying Scotsman' was made non-stop again in 1948 with the A4s once more at the head of the service. Severe floods in the border region saw the service diverted on to the Waverley route which featured particularly difficult gradients and added around 15 miles to the journey. A water stop was thought necessary but a number of the drivers disagreed and kept the train non-stop on several occasions, demonstrating the A4s' economy and the drivers' excellent knowledge of the capabilities.

Shortly after the 1950s began, the A4s were concentrated at King's Cross, Gateshead and Edinburgh Haymarket, which allowed greater care to be taken over the engines' day-to-day maintenance. The locomotives were also rostered to regular drivers and this also helped promote reliability.

As the decade progressed, the A4s were able to repeat the calibre of performances given in the late 1930s and gain a new audience of admirers. Although not working to the same timings or loadings as the 'Coronation', the post-war successor to the LNER's flagship Anglo-Scottish high-speed express was, first the 'Capitals Limited', then in 1953 the 'Elizabethan'. On a number of occasions individual class members claimed extremely long runs of unbroken service during the summer season, with many tales of high speeds and recoveries from delays.

The A4s were also used on named express trains such as the 'Tees-Tyne Pullman', the 'Heart of Midlothian', the 'Talisman' and the 'Fair Maid'. In addition, the A4s were firm favourites on special services and organised outings. No. 60007 *Sir Nigel Gresley* was used for the Stephenson Locomotive Society's jubilee special in mid-1959 and achieved 112 mph which set a post-war speed record for steam traction.

Few outward changes were made to the A4s during their time in service. The first occurred after the start of the Second World War when the side skirting was removed to facilitate access to the motion for oiling and maintenance. In the late 1950s the classmembers not already fitted were recipients of the Kylchap double blastpipe and chimney which greatly improved steaming and reliability for several A4s.

Golden Age Models has produced many of John's A4s, but no. 60010 *Dominion of Canada* and no. 60022 *Mallard* are from L.H. Loveless & Co., whilst no. 60027 *Merlin* is from DJH.

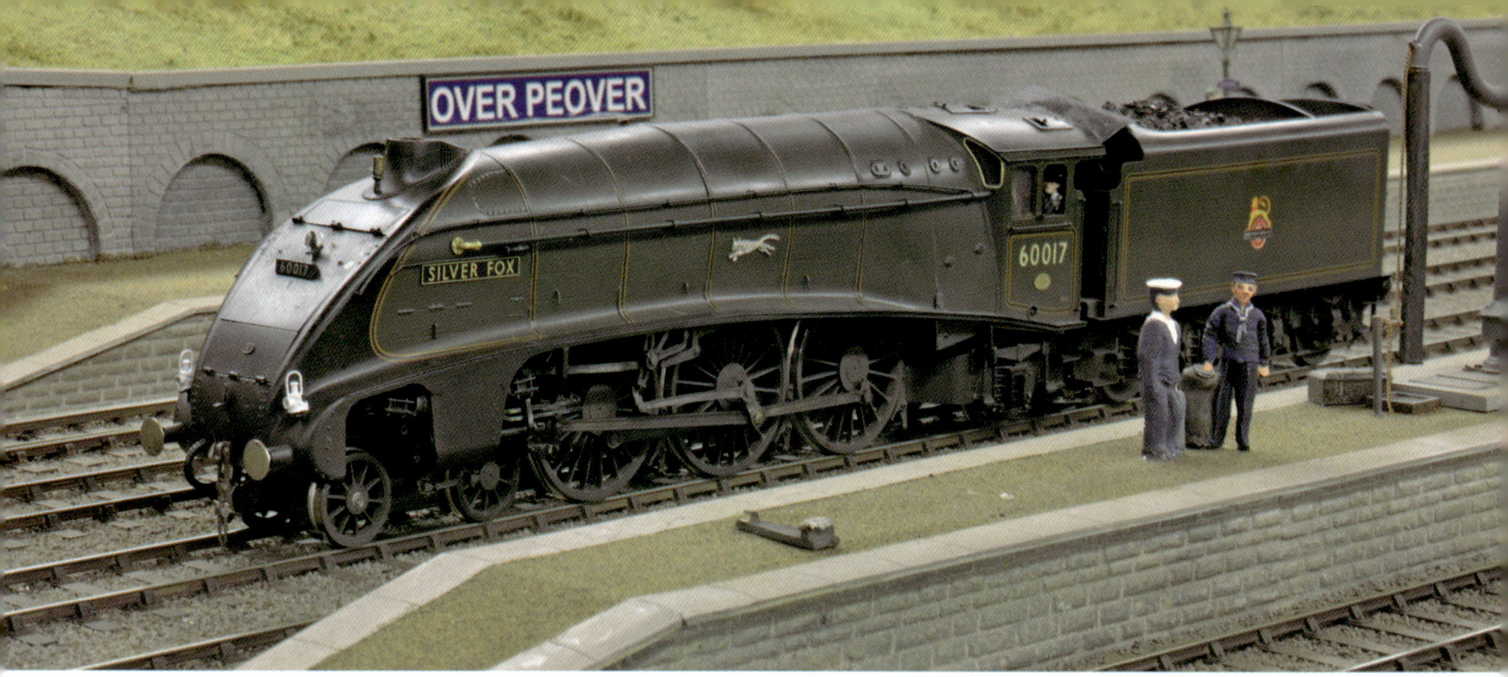
OVER PEOVER
SILVER FOX
60017
60017

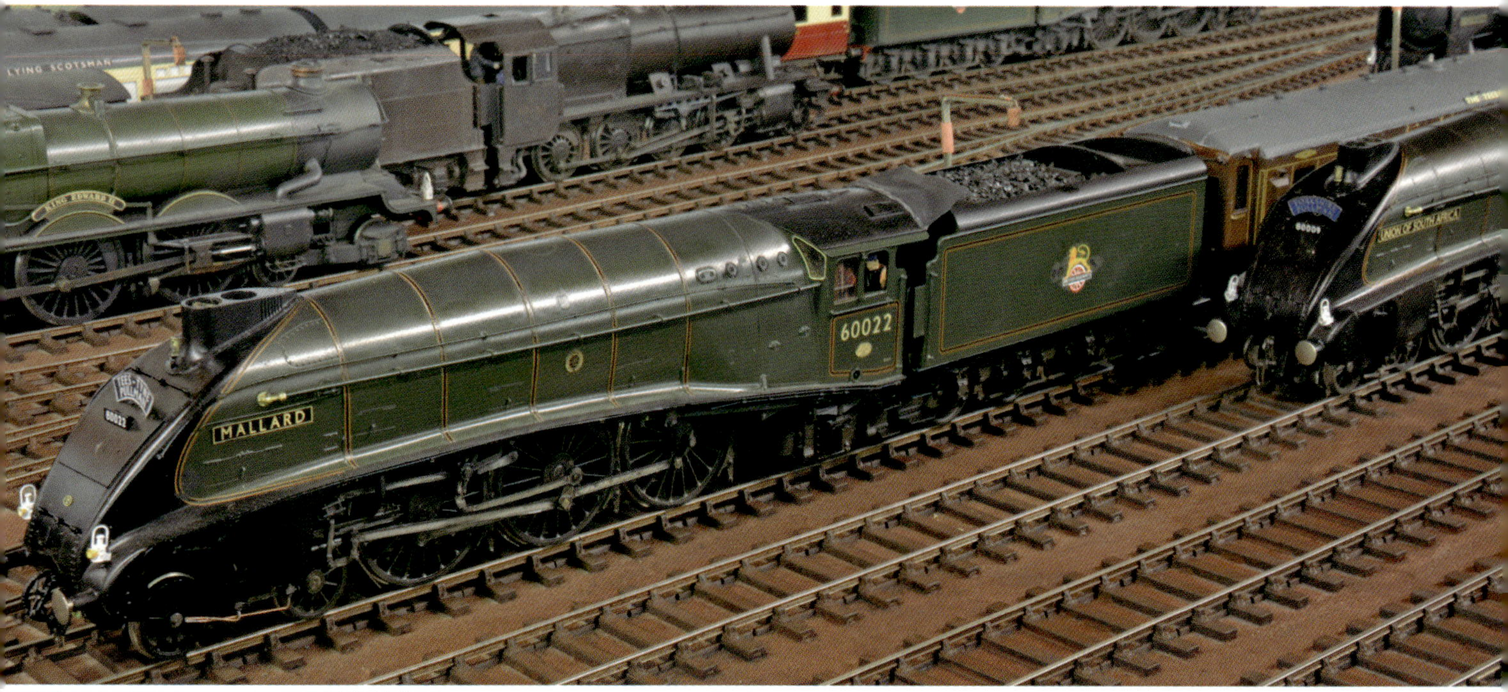
MALLARD
60022
UNION OF SOUTH AFRICA

KINGFISHER
60024
BRITISH RAILWAYS

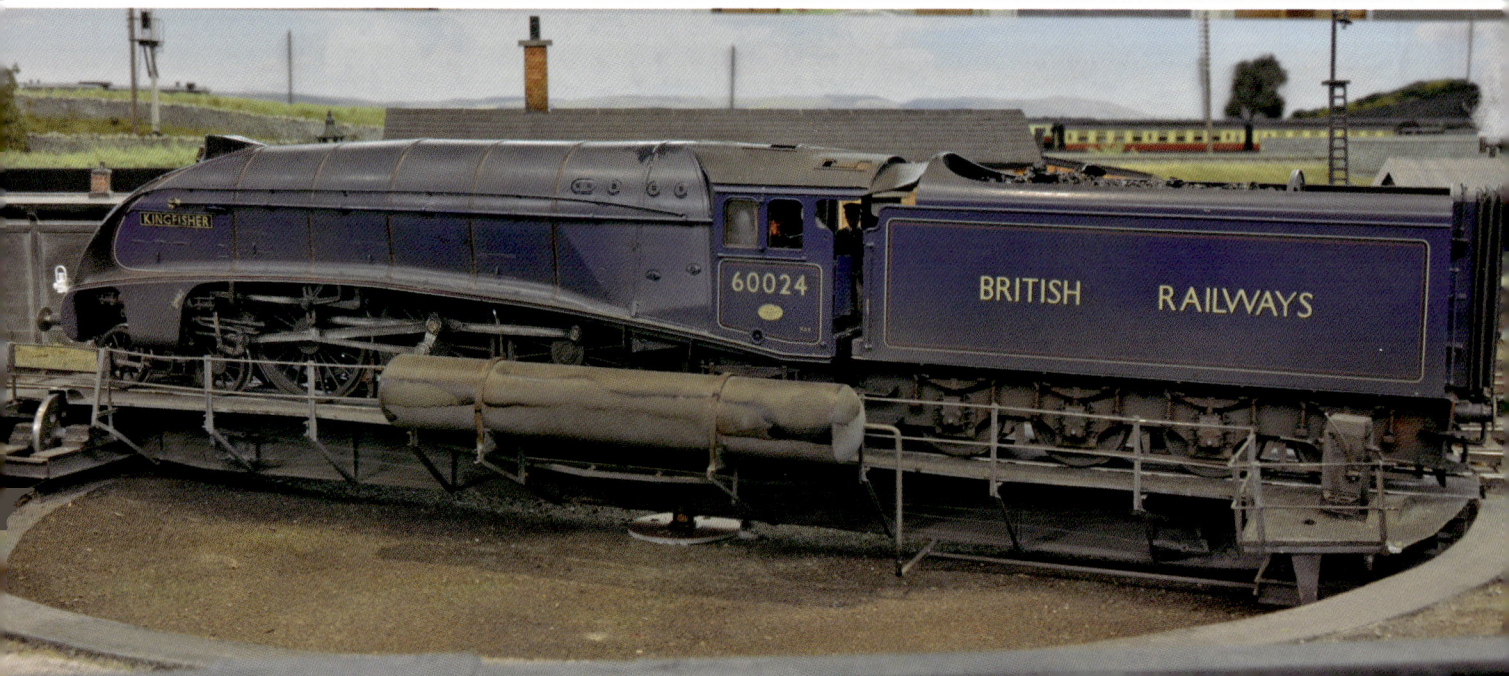

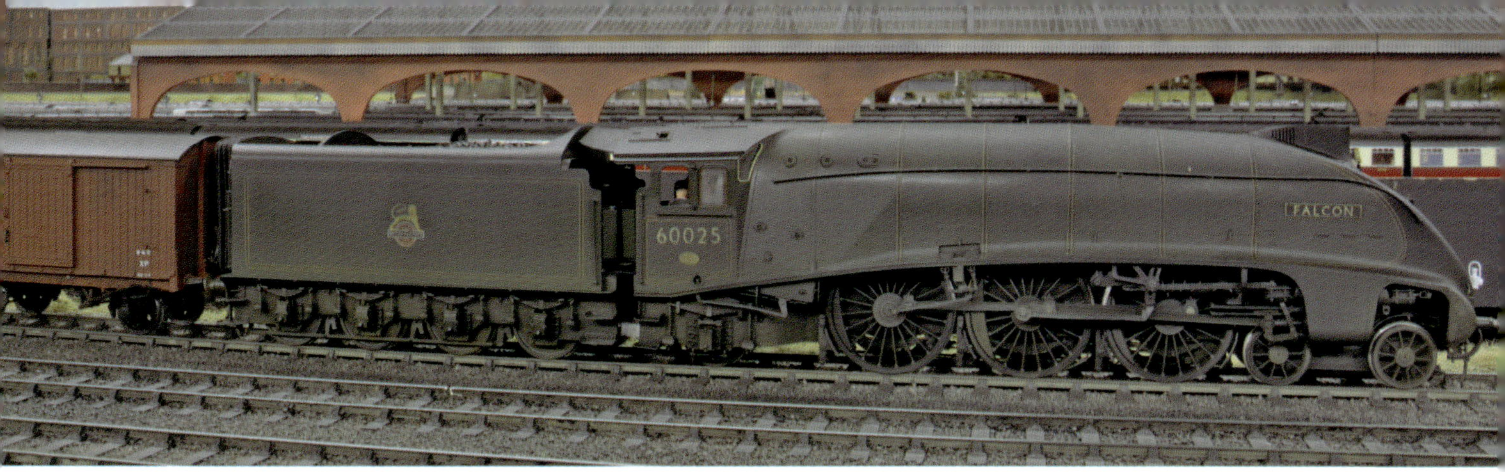
60025
FALCON

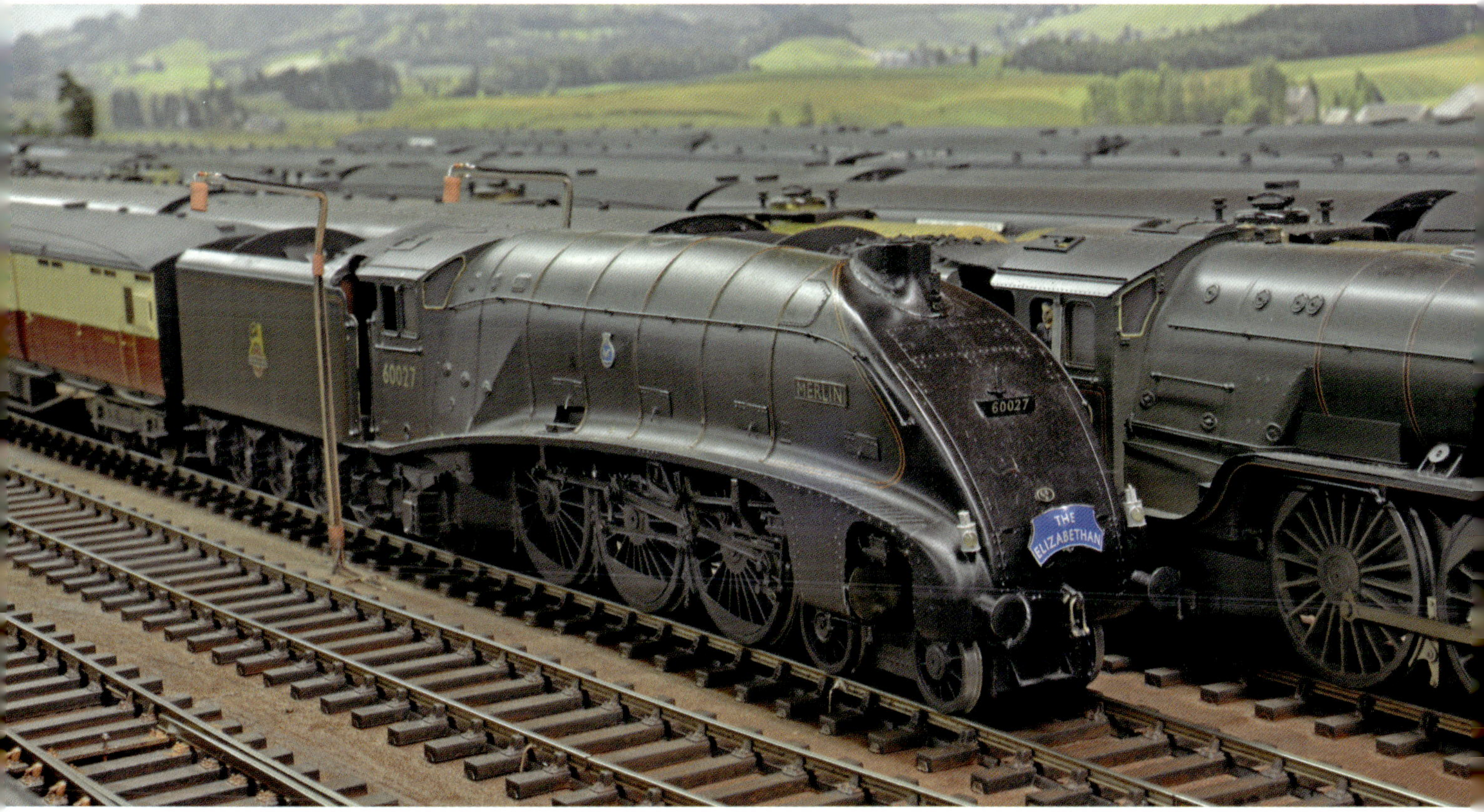
60027
MERLIN
60027
THE ELIZABETHAN

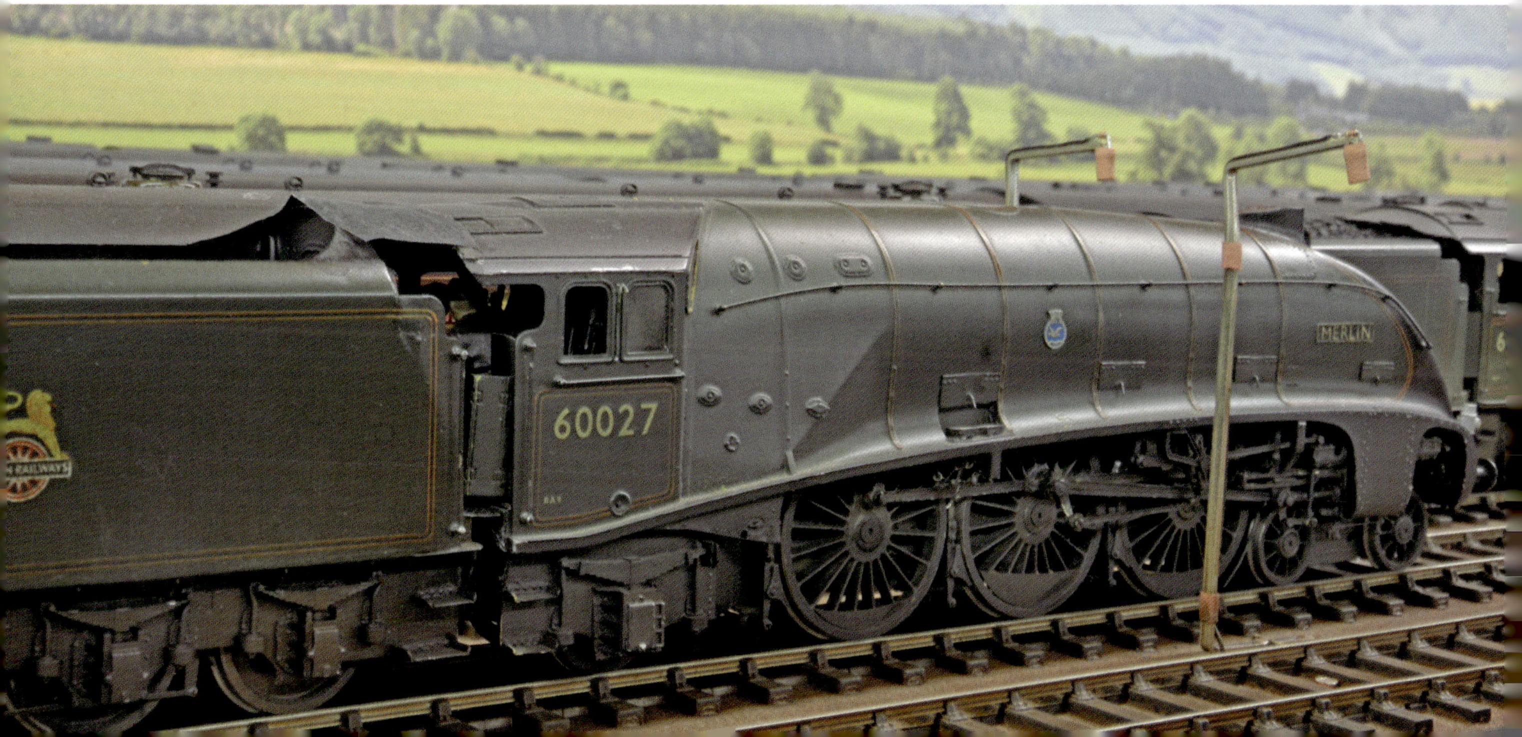
60027
MERLIN

THOMPSON B1 4-6-0

After the death of Gresley, one of Thompson's first acts as the new CME was to produce a design for mixed traffic duties and also had a wide route availability. He chose a 4-6-0 wheel arrangement, two cylinders coupled with 10 in. diameter piston valves and a standard boiler, with simplicity and ease of maintenance at the fore. Ten were built initially over an extended period because of the war before large numbers were ordered from private contractors; by 1950, 410 were in traffic.

The B1s could be found at work on all areas of the LNER, then later the respective regions of BR. Most duties were undertaken by the class and examples could be seen at work on inter-city expresses, suburban trains or goods services.

GRESLEY B17 4-6-0

No. 61657 *Doncaster Rovers* was built at Darlington Works in May 1936 with features that placed the engine in class part four. This meant the engine had a group standard 4,200 gallon tender with space for 7 tons 10 cwt of coal, in addition to a revised cab arrangement as a result, and vacuum braked. Later, the engine would move to class part six when a B1-type diagram 100A boiler was fitted in October 1950.

GRESLEY V2 2-6-2

After the end of hostilities, only one V2 was repainted in LNER lined apple green livery. The rest remained unlined black until going through the works after Nationalisation in 1948. They were then painted gloss black with lining. Latterly, BR green was applied. The V2s originally had all 3 cylinders cast in a Monobloc single casting. Many were later converted to 3 separate cylinder castings and these are identifiable by the more prominent external steam pipes above the cylinders like the A3s. Many consider the V2 to be Gresley's most successful design, and these have pulled trains in excess of 20 coaches. On at least one occasion a single V2 hauled 26 coaches from Peterborough to London. Their 6'2" drivers were particularly suited to the Waverley route with its curves and gradients. When in their final years, some were fitted with Kylchap double blast pipes and were considered the equal of the Pacifics. No. 60800 *Green Arrow* is a FineScaleBrass locomotive, whilst no. 60964 has been constructed from a Martin Finney kit.

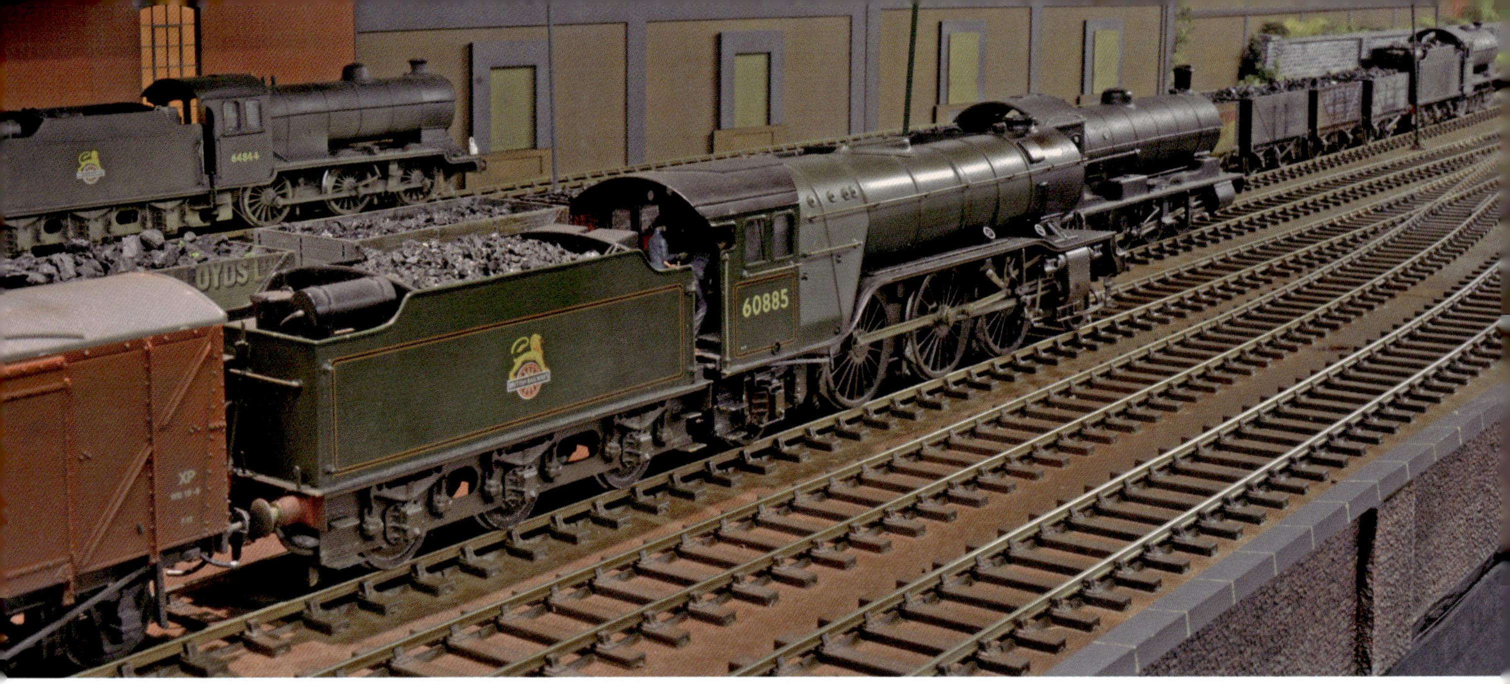
60885

60903

60964
THE DURHAM LIGHT INFANTRY

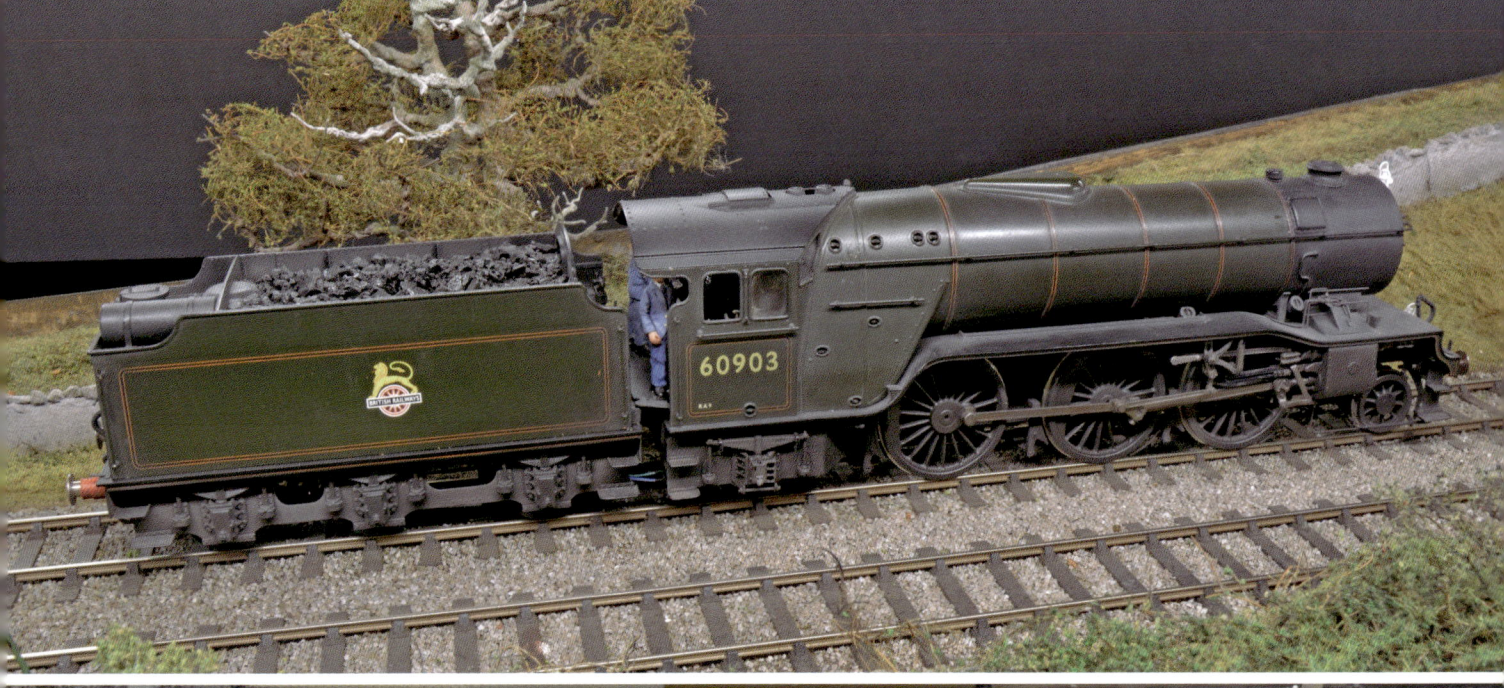

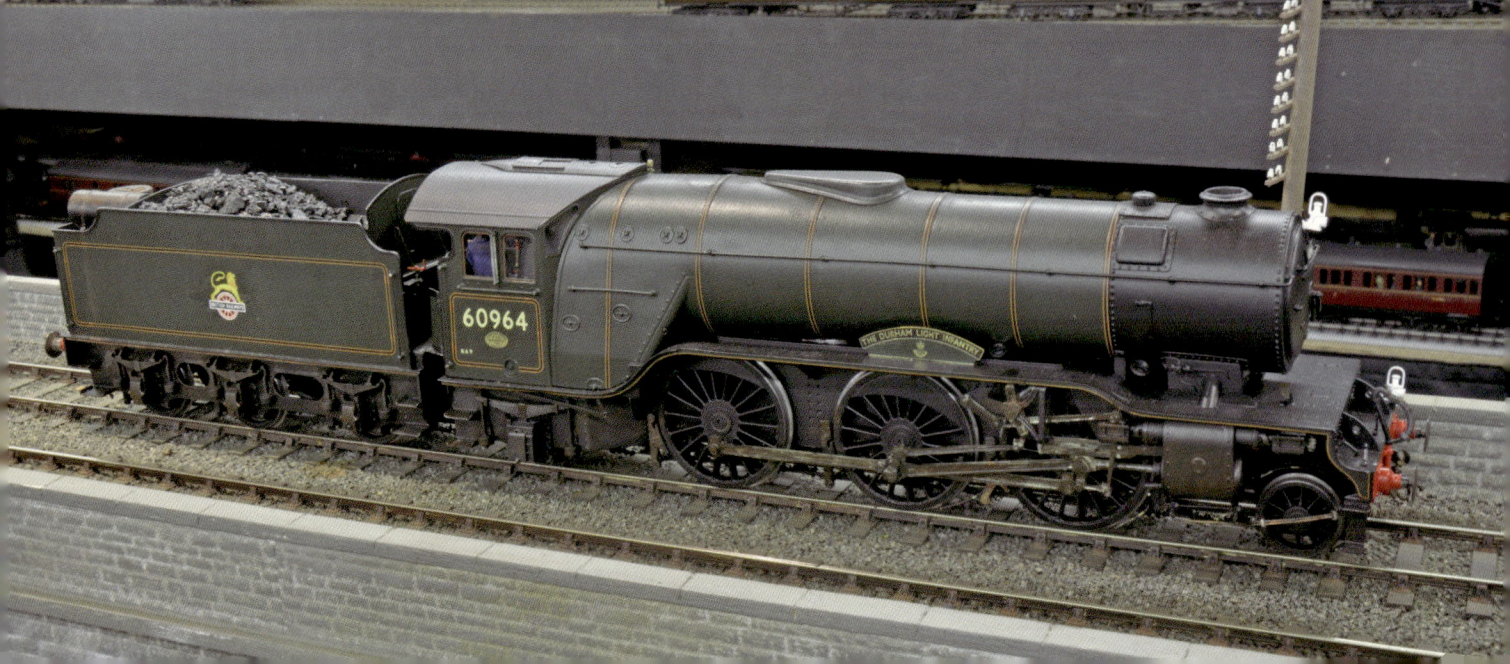

OTHER LOCOMOTIVES

J2 CLASS 0-6-0

No. 65020 was one of just ten J2 Class (GNR J21) 0-6-0s built in 1912 for use on fast main line goods trains. However, the class were soon superseded by Gresley's 2-6-0 design and were transferred to Nottinghamshire and the West Riding where they were used on local passenger and excursion traffic as much as local freight trains.

J39 CLASS 0-6-0

With the introduction of Thompson's B1, the J39 Class had their duties focussed mainly on goods traffic, which became increasingly local as the BR era wore on. No. 64895 was a long-term resident of Carlisle Canal depot after Nationalisation and would have been used on the branches in that area, in addition to freight movements between the many exchange yards around Carlisle. No. 64933 was similarly loyal to Neville Hill shed.

J50 CLASS 0-6-0T

No. 68973, constructed in March 1930, has been modelled in BR livery from a Connoisseur Models kit. The engine has a brass body with a nickel silver chassis. No. 68940 has been completed from a FineScaleBrass kit and is of all-brass construction.

K1 CLASS 2-6-0

Thompson envisaged a new 2-6-0 as part of his standardisation plans and these engines were to replace the J39s on their duties. A prototype was constructed in 1945 and evaluated before an order was placed with the NBLC in 1947. These were slightly altered by Peppercorn from the prototype and appeared in 1949/1950, numbering 70. The K1s were used on the GE Section of the Eastern Region, the North Eastern Region and the Scottish Region at Fort William. The duties at the latter included services on the West Highland lines, whilst in the other areas the class worked mainly freight services.

K2 CLASS 2-6-0

A total of 67 Gresley K2 2-6-0s were built for the GNR (as Class H3) between 1913 and 1921, mainly for use on fast freight services, but also on secondary passenger trains. With the introduction of the K3s, a number of K2s were displaced in the post-Grouping period to constituent areas. A number arrived in Scotland during the late 1920s and early 1930s, including no. 4674, later no. 61764 *Loch Arkaig*. The locomotive was one of several employed at Glasgow Eastfield shed for use on the West Highland Line between Glasgow, Fort William and Mallaig. As a result of this allocation, the loco was named in March 1933, as it was LNER policy to name 13 members of the class which operated the West Highland Line after Scottish Lochs. The austere GN cab was replaced with side-window cab, which protected the crew from the elements, during the following year.

N2 CLASS 0-6-2T

Introduced in 1920 for working suburban passenger trains from King's Cross and Moorgate to stations such as New Barnet and Gordon Hill on the Hertford loop. Articulated quad-art sets were often employed on these. N2s working underground were fitted with condensing gear, and the pipework can be seen on two of John's models, 69523 and 69524. Empty coaching stock was hauled to and from King's Cross and Ferme Park carriage sidings. A small number (13 in 1957) were based in the Edinburgh and Glasgow areas, operating on suburban services.

O2 CLASS 2-8-0

No. 63940 has been erected from a DJH kit and is decorated in BR plain black livery with early emblem. The locomotive was one of many O2s concentrated at Grantham shed after Nationalisation where the main duty was the iron ore traffic from the Highdyke branch to the steelworks in South Yorkshire and Lincolnshire.

V3 CLASS 2-6-2T

With the introduction of Thompson's L1 Class to London suburban services on the Great Eastern section, Gresley V1/V3s at Stratford depot were displaced to Scotland and the North East. Two engines affected by this were nos 67672 and 67680, with both moving to Scotland. The aforementioned was based at Dunfermline, where duties would have taken the engine to Edinburgh, Fife and Stirling, whilst no. 67680 took up residence at Glasgow Eastfield for employment on suburban services and local trains to the coast.

'DELTIC' DIESEL ELECTRIC

With the publication of BR's Modernisation Plan in 1955 the various regions had to find new diesel locomotives to replace their steam classes. Whilst other companies were rushing to their drawing boards, English Electric, which had a number of years' experience with the technology, had produced a prototype diesel electric locomotive featuring a Napier 'Deltic' engine, previously used in marine applications. DP1 was produced in 1955 and at first was tested on the London Midland Region. The engine was rejected as unsuitable, only to be taken on by the Eastern Region, where the 3,300 horsepower at DP1's disposal was considered quite adequate for future services. A production batch of 22 locomotives was subsequently ordered to replace a large number of Gresley Pacifics then at work and appeared between 1961 and 1962. John's model of DP1 was purchased from L.H. Loveless & Co.

CHAPTER FOUR
CARRIAGES

John has amassed an impressive collection of carriages to run behind his many locomotives. The carriages number over 300 examples encompassing the LNER and BR eras. Also included in this time frame are Pullman carriages, which were operated by both entities up and down the East Coast Main Line, and John can boast that he operates more than either the LNER or the Eastern Region.

The LNER period is well represented by many examples of Gresley's teak stock, in addition to the later high speed trains — the 'Silver Jubilee', the 'Coronation' and the 'West Riding Limited'. The precursors to Gresley's streamliners were the Pullman carriages introduced by the LNER shortly after Grouping. The 'Queen of Scots Pullman' and 'Yorkshire Pullman' often travelled faster than the average speeds of the day and offered passengers more comfortable surroundings than generally provided in the company's standard carriages. In spite of this luxury, there were still a number of old GNR six-wheelers in traffic employed on branch line services and several examples are also included in the collection.

The principal services of the BR era were formed from either Thompson coaches or BR's new Mark 1 stock, sometimes supplemented by Gresley's teak vehicles. The 'Flying Scotsman' and the 'Elizabethan' both consisted of Thompson stock during the early 1950s but later had Mk 1 carriages inserted into the formation. The latter became more prevalent as time progressed and could be seen on inter-city services. Both eras feature examples of Royal Mail travelling post office vehicles and other non-passenger carrying stock, while John has a replica of the LNER dynamometer car used on *Mallard*'s famous run of 1938.

Golden Age Models has been the main supplier of the carriages, with all of the Pullman coaches coming from the company, in addition to a number of examples of Gresley's teak stock, whilst others are by Darstaed models. Some of the Mk 1 stock is from Heljan and Peter Cowling. Westdale, Janick, Sparmac, SideLines and the Wagon & Carriage Works models are also represented.

The majority of the carriages have been weathered by John. Other modifications include adding passengers to the interiors of the coaches and capacitors to the coaches fitted with lighting in order to preserve the effect when not in motion. Relevant destination boards have been fitted where necessary.

As the carriage collection is so large — John has duplicate sets for 'up' and 'down' services — the focus of the chapter will be on the named train formations and other interesting sets. Similarly the Pullman cars will not be exhaustively documented, but simply illustrated owing to similarity of design and large numbers.

LNER ERA

'FLYING SCOTSMAN'

Being one of the most prestigious services on the East Coast Main line, the 'Flying Scotsman' was given a dedicated set of carriages. In the LNER era a new train was formed shortly after Grouping and this was partially upgraded for the start of the non-stop service in 1928. New carriages were inserted into the formation at intervals during the 1930s until a new set was deemed desirable for the summer season of 1938. The carriages were built in line with the design of the streamlined sets, featuring sound-proofing, pressure ventilation and improved bogie bearings, but still retained the traditional teak exterior. Built at Doncaster, the train consisted of a brake van, third, first, triplet restaurant/kitchen set, third, buffet, third, first/third composite locker, third brake and third brake.

John's set is comprised from coaches made by Golden Age Models.

'QUEEN OF SCOTS PULLMAN'

Starting life as the 'Harrogate Pullman' shortly after Grouping, in 1928 the service was extended to Glasgow and renamed the 'Queen of Scots'. For the inauguration of this train two new sets of carriages were ordered, consisting of seven vehicles for the 'up' and 'down' services: third brake, third kitchen, third parlour, first kitchen, first parlour, third kitchen and third brake.

The 'Queen of Scots Pullman' set in the collection is from Golden Age Models and has been fitted with a capacitor to keep the interior lights illuminated. Figures have also been added to the interior.

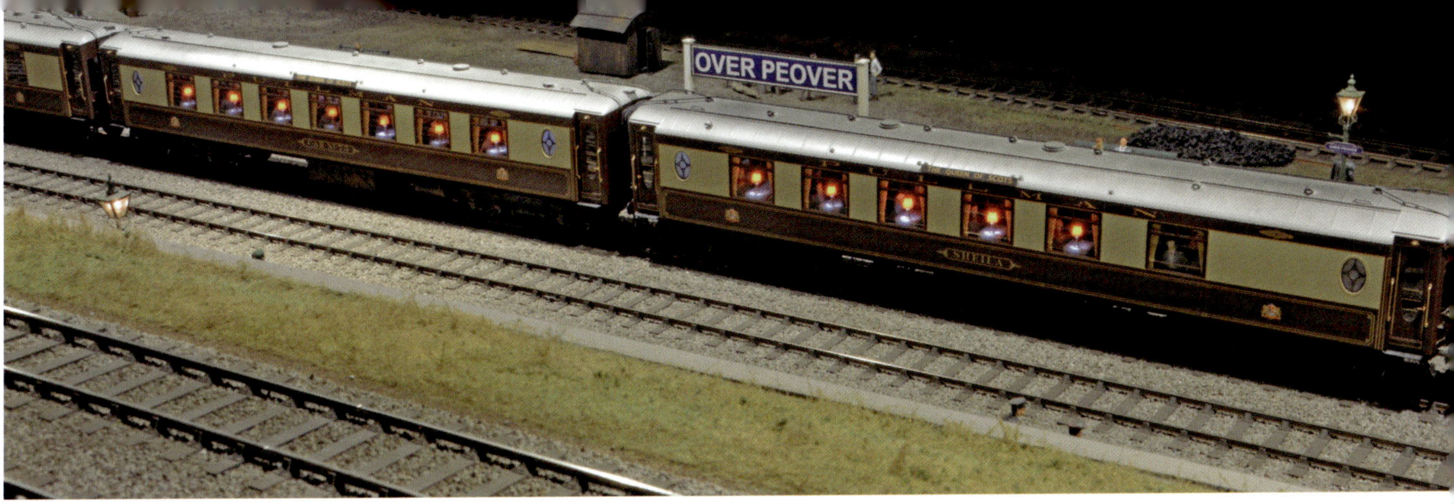
OVER PEOVER

OVER PEOVER

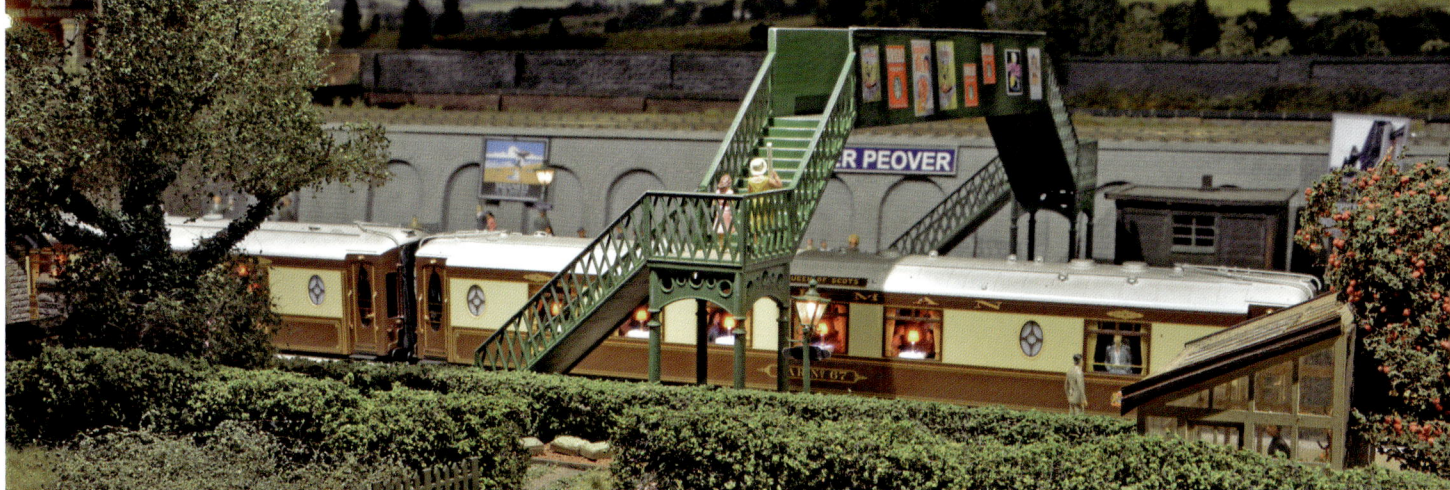

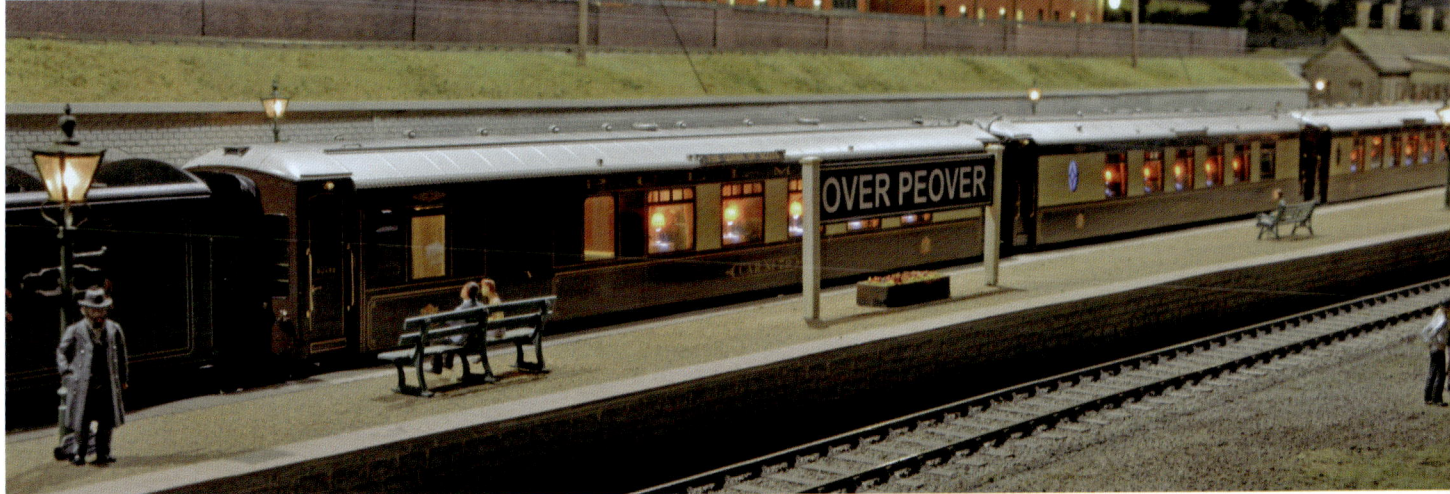

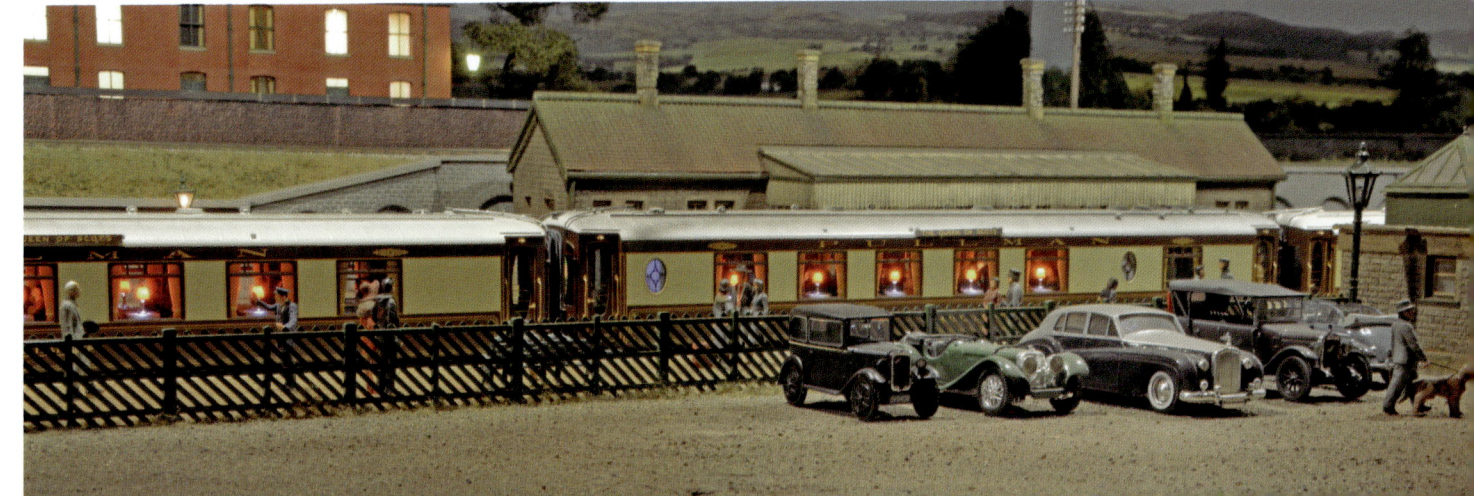

'YORKSHIRE PULLMAN'

The LNER introduced a Pullman service from King's Cross to Sheffield in 1924. Proving unpopular with passengers, even after being extended to Manchester, the train was cancelled in 1925 and the stock redirected to Leeds and Bradford from King's Cross. By the end of the decade the 'West Riding Pullman' was running on to Newcastle, but following the introduction of the 'Silver Jubilee' in 1935 the scope of the service was reduced to Harrogate. At this time the train was renamed the 'Yorkshire Pullman', also featuring a portion for Hull which detached at Doncaster. The set comprised nine vehicles (raised from eight in 1937): third brake, kitchen first, kitchen first, kitchen third, parlour third, kitchen third, brake first, first kitchen, parlour third.

'SILVER JUBILEE'

Ordered from Doncaster Works in February 1935, the 'Silver Jubilee' carriage set comprised seven vehicles arranged in three portions (2-3-2): third brake, corridor third; third restaurant, kitchen, first restaurant; semi-open first and first brake. The coaches differed from traditional practice by employing steel panels for the exterior, which was also covered in Rexine (an artificial leather). The interior noise level was said to have been reduced to just 60 decibels thanks to the placement of asbestos blankets between the interior and exterior panels, in addition to double glazing ¼ in. thick with a ¼ in. air space.

The 'Silver Jubilee' service was quite successful and not long after inauguration the seating arrangements were changed to allow more bookings. From 122 originally, the number of available seats rose to 154 and the train was on average three-quarters full. In 1938 a corridor third was added to the formation, allowing a further 35 passengers to be carried. The new third class vehicle was inserted between the corridor third and brake third.

John's 'Silver Jubilee' set has been bought from L.H. Loveless & Co. and as new was the original seven-carriage formation. The set has been modified to include the 1938 third class carriage.

'CORONATION'

The 'Coronation' carriage set was originally to follow the layout of the 'Silver Jubilee', yet Gresley decided to break the restrictions imposed by the inclusion of restaurant carriages and instead serve meals at the passengers' seats. Therefore, there was a move to 'open' style seating arrangements. The train was arranged from four articulated twin sets: brake third, open third; kitchen third, open third; two open firsts; kitchen third, open brake third. Total seating was for 206 passengers. An unusual addition at the rear of the train was an observation carriage which accommodated sixteen people at a time for one shilling per hour. The shape of the vehicle had been determined in a wind tunnel and complemented the streamlined locomotive at the front. Construction of the carriages was similar to the 'Silver Jubilee' but Rexine was omitted and the exterior was painted Garter blue for the lower panels and Marlborough blue for the upper.

Golden Age Models has supplied both 'Coronation' sets in John's collection.

'WEST RIDING LIMITED'

Whereas the 'Coronation' service began in July 1937, the 'West Riding Limited' did not begin until late September. The schedule was one of the toughest on the LNER, with the Leeds to King's Cross section timed at 2 hours 45 minutes which called for an average speed of 68 mph. The set used the same formation as the 'Coronation' (minus the observation car) and had the same exterior colour scheme; the decor of the interior was changed.

Another set from Golden Age Models, the weathering has been carried out by John.

TOURIST STOCK

In a bid to recapture excursion passengers lost to road transport, the LNER introduced a new set of carriages in 1933. The so-called 'tourist stock' was built economically with plywood and featured a generally sparse interior. One innovation was the introduction of the buffet car which served snacks and drinks in a break from the formality of restaurant carriages. A number of trains were constructed pre-war, and consisted of: two buffet cars, four sets of twin articulated open third, two open brake thirds. John is running a shortened formation, which often occurred during service, and is formed from an open third brake, buffet, two twin open thirds and two open brake thirds at the rear.

EXPRESS TRAIN

Whereas the named and principal expresses were generally new and modern vehicles, other express services were often comprised of dated stock. They could also be non-standard formations that varied from day to day. Here, an express has been formed from ten carriages: brake third, first/third composite, buffet, corridor third, compartment third, corridor third, open third, buffet, open third, third brake. Buffet no. 649 and corridor third no. 4173 are from Janick Models and have been constructed from RJH kits.

A slightly shorter set has recently been assembled following weathering by John. This express comprises: brake third, third, first/third composite, compartment first, compartment third, compartment third, bogie brake.

LOCAL TRAIN

The general pattern of existence for carriages was to begin life on the main line then move down the hierarchy of the various services to end their days on branch line trains. For the LNER, the financial position of the company meant that this process occurred over a longer period of time than would have been desirable and six-wheelers remained in stock for many years. A local train has been created here from a selection of Holden six-wheel stock, including: brake third, third, first/third composite, third.

CHAPTER FOUR – CARRIAGES 141

ROYAL MAIL/ PARCELS

A group of carriages for the conveyance of post/parcels has been assembled at the far side of Castle Cross station. At the rear of the formation is a travelling post office vehicle complete with apparatus for the transfer of mailbags between lineside locations. New vehicles for the Post Office were not provided by the LNER until 1929, followed by several more in 1933. The carriage pictured is from this latter batch (diagram 164) and would have been used on services from King's Cross to York/Newcastle/Edinburgh. Carriages nos 2426 and 2429 are bogie brake vans introduced in 1938 to diagram 245. No. 6739 is a diagram 111 vehicle built for the Great Eastern Section in 1928, having smaller body dimensions than similar carriages.

BR CARRIAGES

'THE ELIZABETHAN'

The 'Capitals Limited' took over from the non-stop 'Flying Scotsman' in 1949 and ran for just four years with a 13-carriage formation. For the coronation of Queen Elizabeth II in 1953 the service was renamed to the 'Elizabethan' and the set was reduced to 11 coaches. These were: bogie van, first, first restaurant, open third, third, third, third, buffet, third, third, brake composite. Here, the set is represented (minus a restaurant first) by models from Ian Kirk, SideLines, Heljan, Easy-Build and Darstaed. The 'Elizabethan' was worked by A4s (due to the need for the corridor connection in the tender for crew changes) to a high standard throughout the train's existence. The train is seen arranged for travelling northward and then the return working.

EXPRESS

An express formation has been created here from: brake third, open third, open third, open third, open third, buffet, corridor first, corridor third, corridor third and corridor brake third. All are Heljan kits.

'TEES-TYNE PULLMAN'

A new Pullman train was introduced in 1948 to serve travellers between King's Cross and Newcastle. This was the 'Tees-Tyne Pullman' which left the north east at 09.00 for arrival at 14.16 and the reverse departed at 17.30 for completion at 22.50. The timings left a lot to be desired and during the following year the service was sped up and this continued incrementally during the 1950s, but still did not reach the timings of the 'Silver Jubilee'. Yet, the service was just as popular and the train comprised nine carriages including the Hadrian Bar. John's set has been purchased from Golden Age Models.

EXPRESS

BR introduced new Mk 1 carriage stock in the early 1950s to replace life-expired examples of the 'Big Four' companies which were still backlogged following the war. These saw the elimination of wood for the structural components of the carriages and metal panels used as standard, with an emphasis being placed on welding techniques and sectional construction. The replacement of old carriages with Mk 1 stock occurred over a long period and examples gradually trickled down from the principal expresses into other services. Here, a short seven-carriage train of mixed-livery stock has been formed to resemble an express or stopping train. The carriages are: corridor brake composite, tourist open second, corridor first, tourist open second, corridor brake composite, corridor first, corridor brake second.

The second train similarly uses Mk 1 coaches, but in the later BR livery and the formation has some different types, namely, a corridor composite and corridor second, whilst sharing the corridor brake second. Both are mainly formed through Westdale kits with a Heljan Mk 1 also included.

STOPPING TRAIN

B1 no. 61005 *Bongo*, which has a stopping train, is held by a signal on the scenic mainline section. The service comprises: corridor composite, corridor composite, corridor second, corridor composite, corridor brake. The set is electrically lit and has been given a light weathering.

SUBURBAN TRAIN

Operating in several areas which required intensive suburban services, the LNER planned for a large-scale replacement of old vehicles following the Second World War. The first coaches appeared in 1947 and were still being built in large numbers during the early 1950s. A set of four carriages is depicted here comprising a diagram 338 lavatory composite, a diagram 339 third, lavatory composite and a diagram 340 third brake.

CHAPTER FIVE
WAGONS

Whilst freight trains are not the primary focus of John's operations, they perform an important secondary role in supporting the atmosphere of the layout, whether this is in the LNER period or the BR era. Therefore, John has assembled a number of impressive formations of wagons that illustrate the various freight services that ran in these time frames.

The LNER inherited a large number of wagons at Grouping, many of these being of wooden construction and without brakes. As time progressed, the company introduced new types with standard dimensions and features to replace older examples. In the main, wagons were built for general purposes, with small numbers for specialised uses. Brakes were fitted to very few vehicles, both old and new, and required brake vans to be coupled to the rear of the train. Although initially building 15-ton brake vans, the LNER quickly decided that 20-ton examples were more desirable and many hundreds of these were built over the ensuing years.

Also running alongside LNER-owned wagons were private owner vehicles. From the outset of the railways, operating companies faced the daunting proposition of providing enough wagons to serve their customers. To reduce costs and improve efficiency, many companies, particularly those dealing with coal, chose to maintain their own fleet of wagons. These were often painted in bright colours and featured the company's name in large lettering on the side as a means of providing free advertising. In the main the wagons were constructed from wood and met the Railway Clearing House specifications set by the railway companies.

Following the outbreak of war in 1939, private owner wagons were requisitioned by the government for the duration and in the event were retained and taken over by British Railways. In total the company had almost 1.3 million wagons in 1948, all being of varying age and condition. BR decided on a policy to repair modern vehicles and replace older ones. The latter was done on a relatively large scale and favoured the use of metal in place of wood, with improved lubrication for axleboxes, but the use of brakes was still confined to certain types.

The models representing these many variations are from several manufacturers: Parkside Dundas, Dapol, Slater's, Skytrex Model Railways and Lionheart Trains. All have been given varying degrees of weathering by John, whilst the brake vans have been upgraded to carry illuminated tail lights and some have a figure representing the guard.

As with the previous chapter, all of the collection will not be covered due to volume and repetition of types, instead focussing on relevant sets of wagons and interesting individual examples.

LNER ERA

VAN TRAINS

Covered goods vans were favoured by the LNER as the type offered better protection to merchandise being transported. Initially, these were of 12 tons capacity, all wood construction and had a 9ft wheelbase, with some fitted for brakes and others not. Large numbers were built up to the early 1930s when the design was changed to feature pressed steel ends and 10 ft wheelbase, which was deemed more desirable as greater stability at higher speeds was offered. Whilst many vans were built for general goods, high quantities were also introduced for specialised traffic, such as fruit, fish and meat.

The first train is mainly comprised of insulated fish vans, but other vans are also present. Serving several ports, the LNER catered for fish traffic with vans of 10 tons capacity, of wooden construction with sliding doors and vacuum brakes. Another has been formed from vans of various vintages and also includes an LMSR banana van. Most of the vans are from Parkside Dundas and have been heavily weathered.

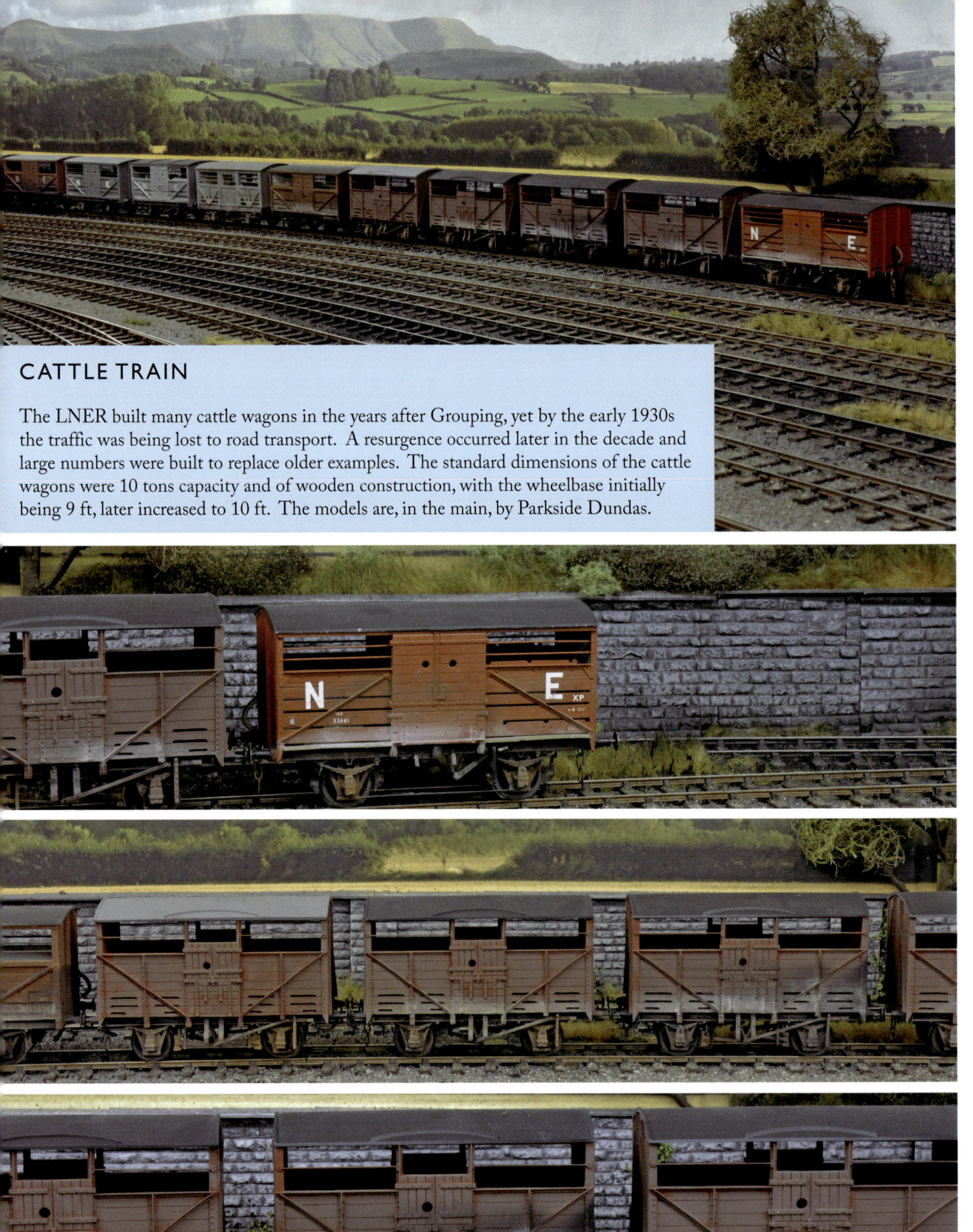

CATTLE TRAIN

The LNER built many cattle wagons in the years after Grouping, yet by the early 1930s the traffic was being lost to road transport. A resurgence occurred later in the decade and large numbers were built to replace older examples. The standard dimensions of the cattle wagons were 10 tons capacity and of wooden construction, with the wheelbase initially being 9 ft, later increased to 10 ft. The models are, in the main, by Parkside Dundas.

MIXED FREIGHT

A number of Great Western Railway wagons, in addition to a London Midland & Scottish Railway open wagon, have been mixed together with several private owner wagons to form this train. Wagons from other railway companies would often cross over into 'foreign' territory to reach their final destination. Examples of model manufacturers included in this train are: Skytrex, H.C. Bull & Co. Ltd; Parkside Dundas, GWR goods van; Slater's, Walkers tank wagon.

COAL TRAINS/WAGONS

Serving several mining areas, coal traffic was very important to the LNER. Although private owner wagons were favoured to transport the product by pre-Grouping companies, the LNER chose to increase the number of coal wagons owned by the company. Several variations were erected in the inter-war years, but the main type was of 12-tons capacity with a seven-plank side and 9ft wheelbase, conforming to RCH specifications. Other examples of coal wagon erected by the LNER included hopper wagons of 12/13/20 tons capacity and steel coal wagons which appeared from the mid-1930s onwards.

Several types of LNER coal wagon are present in John's collection and run alongside the private owner wagons, many of which are models from Slater's. Others are by Skytrex, whilst a recent addition to the fleet has been the Bullcroft coal wagons, which have been purchased from Pete Waterman. The private owner wagons are mainly from collieries in Yorkshire, but there are some from further afield.

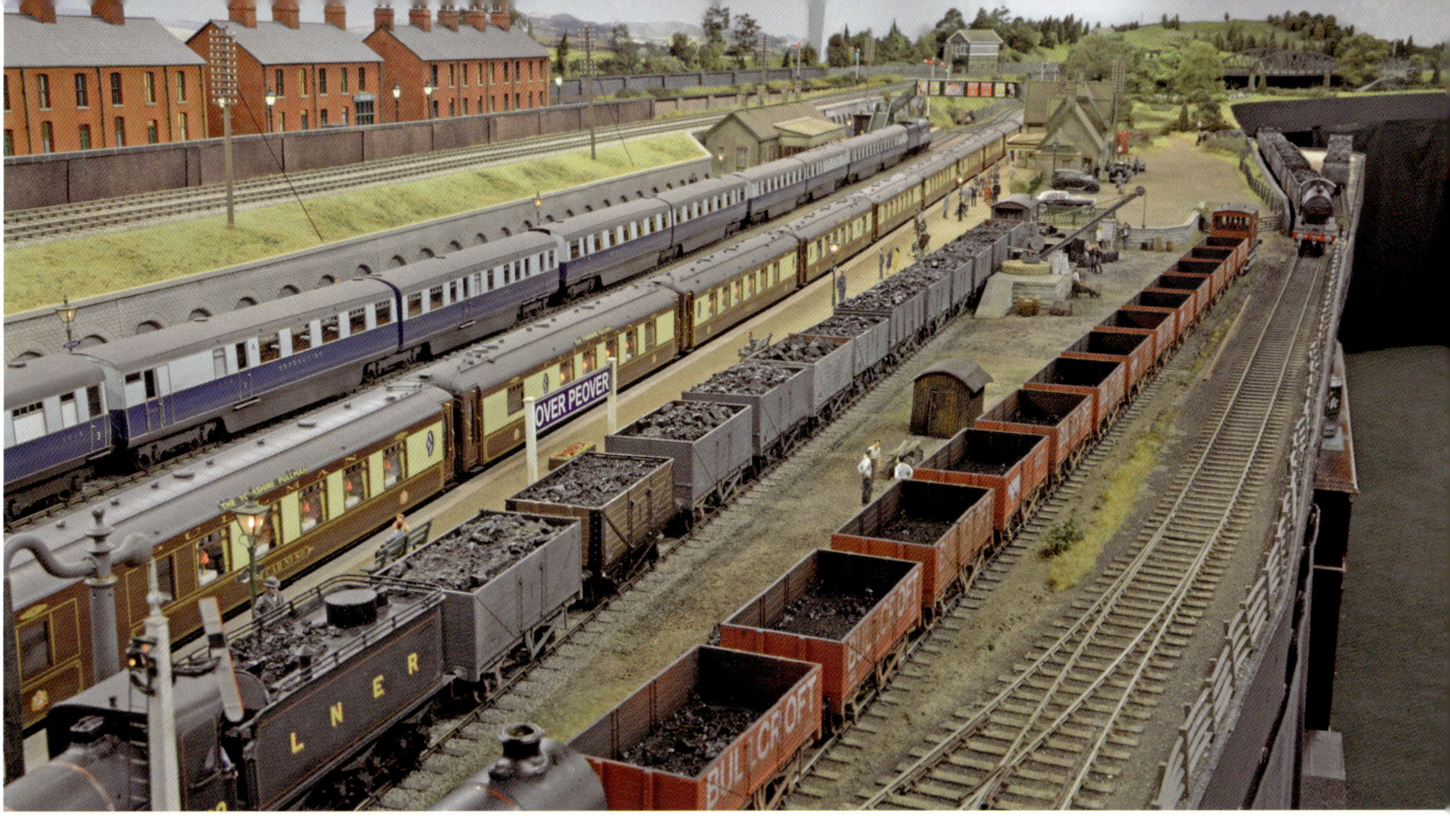
OVER PEOVER
L N E R
BULLCROFT

THE YORKSHIRE PULLMAN
CAR Nº 80

OVER PEOVER

SHEILA

N E

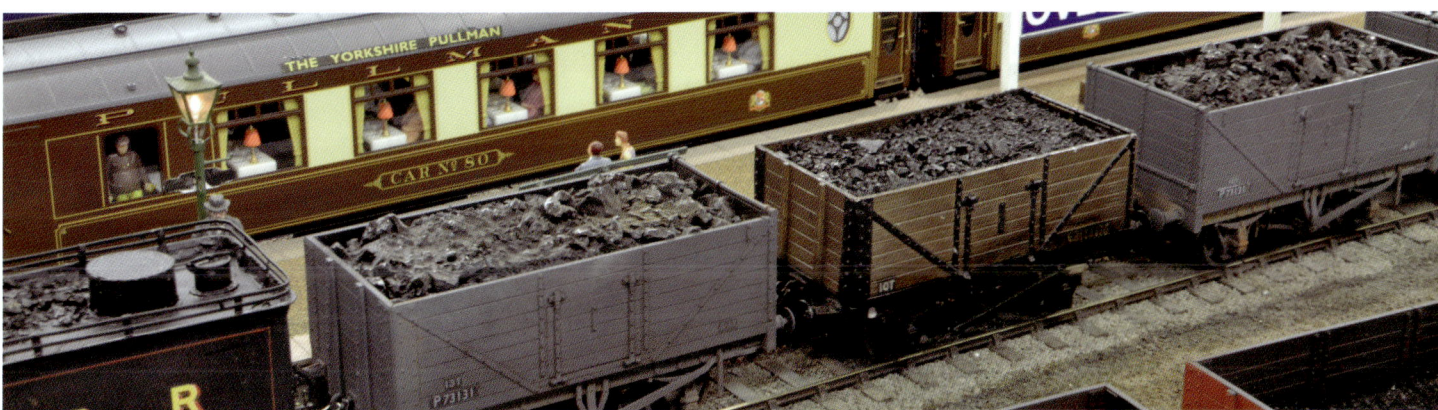

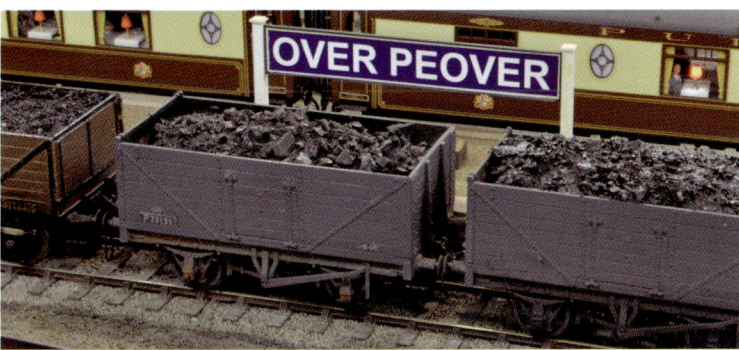

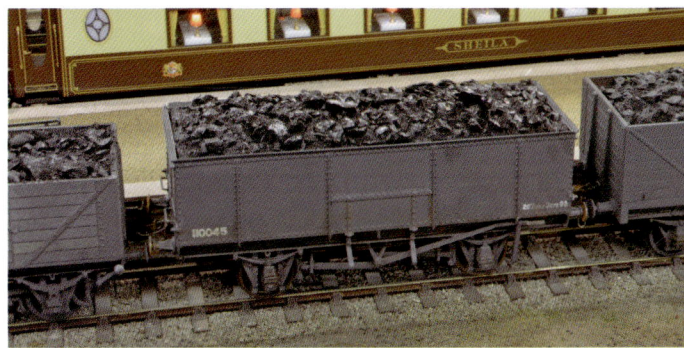

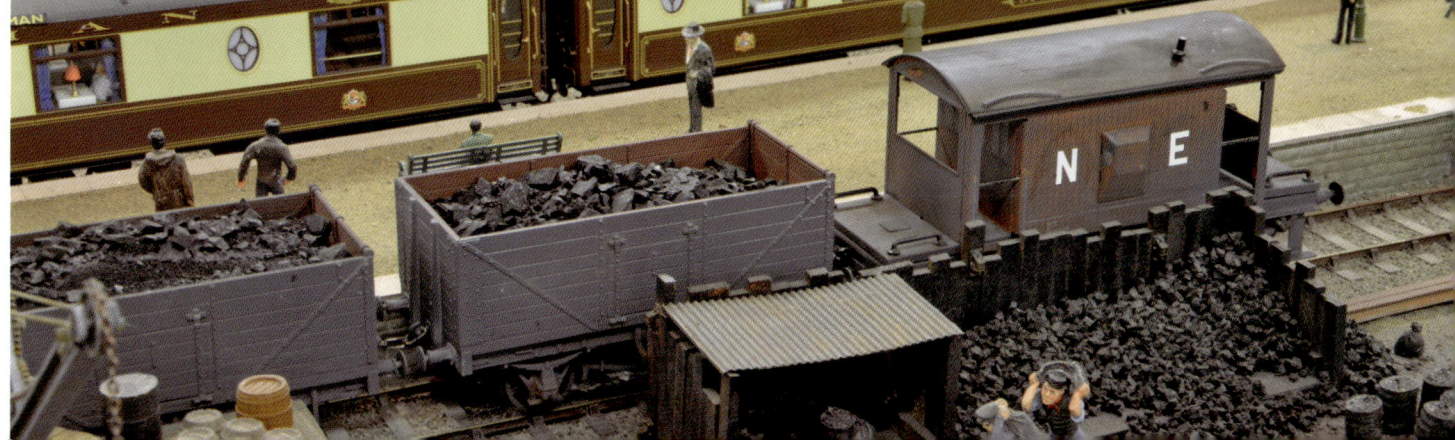

MIXED FREIGHT

This train mainly consists of well wagons and multiple bolster wagons, but there are also examples of alumina wagons. The former were primarily used for the transportation of heavy objects to and from the heavy industrial areas of the LNER, such as the North East. Bulk alumina was also a traffic that the company catered for with specially constructed wagons. The types in this train were converted by the LNER from old 20-ton hopper wagons formerly used to convey coal. Slater's have created the kit used to build them, in addition to the 20-ton brake van, and the Weltrol is by Darstaed.

PLATE WAGONS

With the LNER serving steel mills in South Yorkshire and the North East, wagons were provided for the movement of steel plates. The four-wheel examples had a capacity of 12 tons and were constructed from steel with a 15 ft wheelbase. The wagons were also useful for other traffic, such as the movement of large items which were perhaps too big for the smaller low-sided wagon. These plate wagons are from Parkside Dundas, but the goods being transported are aftermarket items.

BR PERIOD

MIXED FREIGHT

During the 1950s, BR introduced new wagons to replace life expired vehicles and these mingled with older stock that was deemed still worthy of revenue-earning service. Here, several examples of BR's designs are seen as part of mixed freight services along with ex-LNER wagons in two trains. The first is short and comprised two 16-ton all-steel mineral wagons, 12-ton van, BR 12-ton van and ex-LNER fish van. The second train is headed by an LNER 50-ton brick wagon followed by a BR 12-ton pipe wagon, an ex-GWR 12-ton van, a tank wagon, a milk tank, two BR Weltrol WHs and an LNER Flatrol E.

VAN TRAIN

As with the mixed freight, the two van trains featured consist of mixed BR and 'Big Four' stock. BR followed the precedent set before Nationalisation in building covered vans instead of open wagons. Furthermore, the 10 ft wheelbase was continued and large numbers were fitted with vacuum brakes allowing the vans to run in express formations. Nearly all were constructed with pressed steel ends with wooden bodies; some possessed plywood sides.

COAL WAGONS

BR built coal wagons in great numbers following Nationalisation. These were of 16 tons capacity with end doors and of all-steel construction; many were fabricated through welding rather than riveting. The move away from wood had begun in the late 1930s and continued during the war due to greater durability and ease of maintenance of metal. A number of examples of BR 16-ton coal wagons can be seen amongst several formations which also include wooden wagons that would still have been present during the 1950s as they were yet to be replaced.

PETROL TANK

BR built few tank wagons and those companies needing such vehicles had to obtain their own from private contractors. Pictured here is an example of a Shell petrol tanker which forms part of a larger train of the same stock. The tankers were obtained from Darstaed, which produced a run of the type in 2015 in several liveries.

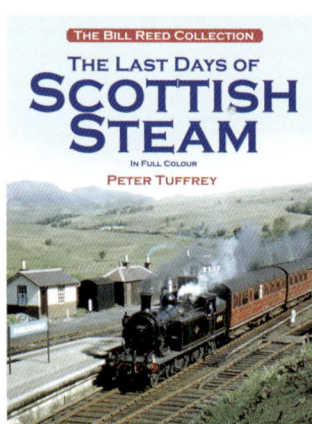

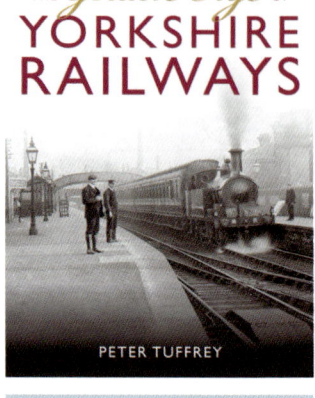
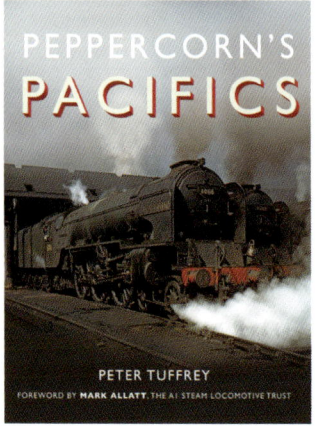
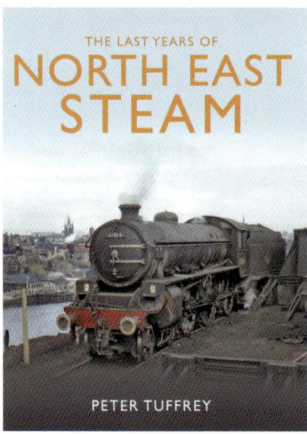
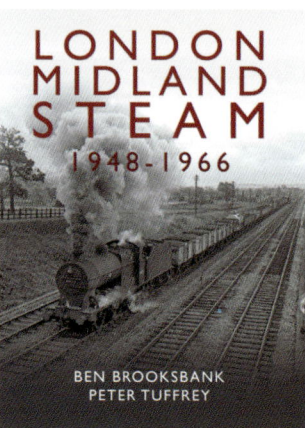
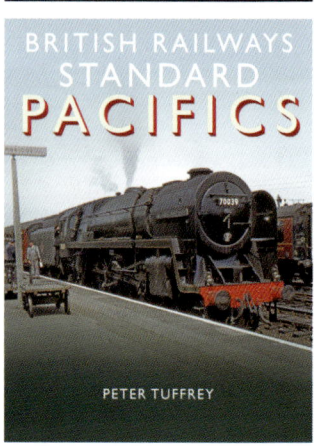

Also available from Great Northern by Peter Tuffrey

The Last Days of Scottish Steam

The Last Years of Yorkshire Steam

Gresley's A3s

The Golden Age of Yorkshire Railways

Peppercorn's Pacifics

The Last Years of North East Steam

London Midland Steam 1948-1966

British Railways Standard Pacifics

visit *www.greatnorthernbooks.co.uk* for details.